PARD OMAR

DC 2011.

What people are saying about
Three Minutes to Success

When it comes to helping entrepreneurs grow their businesses, no one does it with greater efficiency than Jim Blasingame. In every chapter of Three Minutes To Success, *Jim delivers maximum message with a minimum of words. Don't just buy this book–practice this book.*

—**Jay Mincks**
Executive Vice President, Sales and Marketing of Administaff

In Three Minutes To Success, *Jim Blasingame helps you hit the ball of success—hard. There's much to learn here—leadership, idea generation, trust, training, self-analysis—you get the picture. And here's the bonus: Jim makes it easy to read. Good job, Jim*

—**Robert Dilenschneider**
President, The Dilenschneider Group
Author of *A Time For Heroes*

Jim Blasingame has done it again! Three Minutes to Success *blends a wry sense of humor, down-to-earth common sense, real-life anecdotes and a unique insight into what business people really need to know to make their way through the business jungle. It's like having a friend and consultant at your side along the way.*

—**Russell Lee Brown**
Author of "BizPricer: Business Valuation Software"

Again, Jim Blasingame has proven why he is "The Voice of Small Business." Not only is Three Minutes to Success *written in a compelling and lively style, but it's packed with topics that small business owners face every day. He even quotes Warren Zevon. Now, that's my kind of entrepreneur! Kudos to Jim for speaking our language while saving us time. Goodonya, Jim.*

—**Jeffery Zbar**
Chief Home Officer
Author of *Teleworking & Telecommuting*

With Three Minutes To Success, *Jim Blasingame hits the ball right down the middle of the fairway of essential business principles. You can't go wrong with the management keys you'll find in Jim's new book, but you certainly can without them. Any one of the concepts Jim delivers will help you find more profit and greater success.*

—**Steven C. Martin**
President, Business Solutions - The Positive Way
Author and profitability expert

Like a great coach, Jim teaches us that there are no shortcuts to success. In his newest book, Three Minutes To Success, *Jim defines a truly successful business as one that does not just make you lots of money, but also provides invaluable relationships, with employees, customers and others, that can last a lifetime. As Jim would say, you can write that on a rock.*

—John Fox, Esq.
Author of *If Americans REALLY Understand the Income Tax*

On his talk show, Jim Blasingame interviews top experts, collecting the most telling truths and principles about running a small business. Now he's laid them out for us in a simple grab-and-go format. Three Minutes to Success *will save gangs of small business owners heaps of time and trouble.*

—Jim Ballard
Author of *Mind Like Water*

Three Minutes To Success *is a small business "Declaration of Independence," written by Jim Blasingame. Jim holds these "truths" to be self evident, so that every entrepreneur can pursue life, liberty, happiness and success. I'm grateful Jim has made small business his passion and has compiled 52 habits of effective small business.*

—Mike Menzies
President, Easton Bank and Trust

In Three Minutes To Success, *Jim Blasingame delivers to small business owners valuable insights and strategies on improving their entrepreneurial skills. Jim's down-to-earth enthusiasm, coupled with his comprehensive prescriptions for success, makes this a "must read" for every small business owner.*

—Giovanni Corotolo
Director, Small Business Policy, U.S. Chamber of Commerce

It will only take you three minutes to realize that you've picked up a gem of a book! The simple and inspiring messages Jim Blasingame offers in his new book, Three Minutes To Success, *are easy to grasp and yet so powerful in their consequences.*

—Tom Asacker
Branding expert
Author of *A Clear Eye for Branding*

If you're looking for the keys to small business success and don't have a lot of time, congratulations. Jim Blasingame's new book is just what you're looking for. You'll keep this book on your desk, not on the shelf. Well done, Jim.

—Marc Allen
Author of *The Millionaire Course*

Jim Blasingame's new book puts into thoroughly tasty bite-size pieces the banquet of small business fundamentals.

—**Barbara Weltman, Esq.**
Author of *The Complete Idiot's Guide to Starting an eBay Business*

Wise and pithy wisdom about the key issues facing every small business. Jim delivers essential entrepreneurial perspectives and practical tools and tips as only he can.

—**Gene Griessman**
Author of *The Words Lincoln Lived By*

If you have three minutes to invest, Jim Blasingame's new book is one of the very best places you could ever spend them. Wise, witty, and full of useful advice. Count on Jim to give you a wonderful return for your investment.

—**Peter Meyer**
Author of *Creating and Dominating New Markets*

Whether on-the-air or in-print, Jim Blasingame talks about business like someone who's signed the front of paychecks. He's a wealth of wisdom for entrepreneurs competing in the global markets of the 21ˢᵗ century.

—**Steve Del Bianco**
President, NetChoice.org

Three Minutes to Success *is a necessity for anybody on the front lines of small and medium business. It's full of common sense and real-world experience boiled down to a powerful core. Jim Blasingame has a true gift for getting to the heart of entrepreneurship.*

—**Tim Berry**
President, Palo Alto Software

Three Minutes to Success *is classic Jim Blasingame—practical, eye-opening, witty and fun, with no punches pulled. You'll feel like you're sitting down with a mentor for lunch and a chat about where you're going to take your business.*

—**Don Sadler**
Vice President, Media Three Publications

Jim Blasingame provides a variety of lessons, with immediately applicable tools, designed to help any small business owner improve both entrepreneurial strategy and tactics. Jim's lessons break small business operations into readily defined tasks and include helpful examples along the way. The overall effect is a book any small business owner should keep within arm's reach.

—**Patricia Greene, Ph.D.**
Dean of Undergraduate School, Babson College

If you want to study the theory of entrepreneurship, enroll in a college. If you want to BE an entrepreneur, read what Jim Blasingame writes and listen to what he says. Three Minutes to Success *is the launching pad for your next entrepreneurial step.*

—Dan Poynter
Author of *The Self-Publishing Manual*

In Three Minutes to Success, *Jim takes a fresh approach to sharing key business lessons without sacrificing quality or content. Time is an entrepreneur's most precious commodity, and Jim's 52 nuggets of wisdom is an efficient tool for small business owners to turn to for practical guidance and inspiration.*

—Karen Kerrigan
President & CEO, Small Business & Entrepreneurship Council

Three Minutes To Success *is another reason why I trust Jim Blasingame more than any other small business source in America. This book has the capacity to save you years of expensive trial and error and is an absolute must for anyone who leads, owns or works in a small business—plus anyone thinking of starting a small business. Jim Blasingame really is "the voice of small business."*

—Arky Ciancutti, M.D.
Co-author of *Built On Trust*

After reading Jim's incredible new book, I'm going to load up on some of his rocks (52). "Write this on a rock," that is. My favorite is Reinvention or Extinction — the choice is yours, but I'm sure you'll find one..

—Ken Leebow
Author of *300 Incredible Things to Do on the Internet* book series

Only Jim Blasingame would have the audacity to say he could teach you a success tip in three minutes, but he's also the only person I know who can actually do that. Dizzy Dean said, "It ain't bragging if you can do it." In Three Minutes To Success, *Jim does it.*

—Ivan Misner
Founder & CEO, Business Network International, Inc.

Jim Blasingame has done it again! Another great source of wisdom and insight for America's small business owners from a great American and THE advocate of small business. Who else could pack 52 of the handiest small business pearls into one great book? Way to go, Jim!

—Andrew Sherman, Esq.
Author of *Franchising and Licensing*

Jim Blasingame

Three Minutes to Success

*52 classic small business lessons
you can read in 3 minutes*

Three Minutes to Success

52 classic small business lessons
you can read in 3 minutes

Publisher's Cataloging-In-Publication Data
(Prepared by The Donohue Group, Inc.)

Blasingame, Jim.
  Three minutes to success : 52 classic small business lessons you can read in 3 minutes / Jim Blasingame.
    p. ; cm.
  Includes bibliographical references.
  ISBN-13: 978-0-9709278-1-1

  1. Small business—Management. 2. Entrepreneurship.
  3. Success in business. 4. New business enterprises. I. Title.

HD62.7 .B556 2006
658.022   2005907464

10 9 8 7 6 5 4 3 2 1

This book is dedicated to my children,
Jenny and Craig,
who both continually do things
that make me look like a good father.

Also by Jim Blasingame

Small Business is Like a Bunch of Bananas

Table of Contents

Three Minutes to Success ...

Acknowledgements

A book is essentially a complicated jigsaw puzzle, the ultimate beauty of which is made manifest by a community of contributors who work without the benefit of a picture on the box cover.

The primary puzzler—in this case, the author—is responsible for the overall result, but is indebted to his or her community of co-puzzlers, each of whom shine their particular light of expertise on the work and make it more excellent than would have been possible by the author alone.

There is no confusion about whom this author depends upon for primary, secondary, and tertiary support. Davonna, you continue to bless me by sharing life and work with me. Thank you for always knowing when to be my critic, when to be my safe harbor, and when to just let me be. As always, this work belongs to you, too.

To Jim O'Brien, thanks for your abiding support and friendship.

To Sarah Gilliland and Bliss Bowman, two important members of the SBN team, thanks for your daily support of my efforts.

Thanks to our business's best friends, our bankers at First Metro Bank.

After my parents, no one contributed more to my recalcitrant development into productive adulthood than the dozens of long-suffering teachers and professors. Thanks to all those who played a part in my acquisition of knowledge.

Since space prevents a listing of all of my teachers, I've made a practice of singling out two in each book. To my fourth and fifth grade teachers, Michael Luketic and James O'Donnell, thanks for your commitment to educating even those who required significant corporal remediation. And contrary to your prophecies those many years ago about how I might turn out, I have not done any jail time, so far.

To the hundreds of members of my Brain Trust—the experts who join me on my talk show—thank you for your constant examples of what excellence looks like. Nothing I do or create is without some influence by each of you.

There are certain members of The Brain Trust whom I would like to identify and thank for their specific contribution: Burton Folsom, Don Sadler, Russell Brown, Tom Asaker, Tim Berry, Steve Del Bianco, Bob Dilenschneider, Barbara Weltman, Joan Pryde, Ivan Misner, Dan Poynter, Joan Avagliano, Steve Martin and Steve Forbes.

Thanks for always being there when I need an ear, a critical eye, or a valuable opinion. You guys rock!

Thanks to Zach Kallenbach and Doc Giffin for your strategic assistance and support.

Of course, I must thank the man who has contributed the Foreword for this book. Mr. Palmer, you've been one of my heroes for decades because of how you conduct yourself both on and off the golf course. To be associated with you in any way is an honor beyond my ability to adequately express in words, so I'll just say, thank you, sir.

And, finally, to once again paraphrase Winston Churchill, I must thank the few who do so much for so many: small business owners. Your commitment, courage and spirit continues to inspire me. You are my heroes.

Jim

Foreword

When you think about it, a golf professional trying to make a living on one of the tours is the ultimate small business owner.

They have to learn as much as they can about the fundamentals of their profession, practice those fundamentals religiously, try as hard as they can when they go to work, and find a way to outperform their formidable competition. And then, since there are no guarantees, they might be successful.

Sounds just like you, doesn't it?

Working without a net, you strike out on your own to follow the dream of making a place for yourself and your business in the marketplace. You know that if you don't offer products and services that customers will buy, and then collect your money and make a profit, you don't get to keep doing what you love.

The reason I know so much about these folks is because, as you may know, I've been a professional golfer—and a small business owner—now for over 50 years.

Ever look into the eyes of a touring golf pro? It's the same look I've seen in the eyes of so many small business owners over the years. It's a look that ranges from excitement about the possibility of pursuing a dream, to determination forged by faith in oneself, to resolve tempered by the understanding that if they don't perform well in a field of competition, they don't get paid.

That's why two of my favorite kinds of people are touring golf pros and small business owners. And it's why I was pleased when Jim Blasingame asked me to provide the foreword for this excellent book.

If you know anything about my career, you know I've been blessed with some degree of success. But just like you, from the time I began my career right up to today, I've had no guarantees. So for the next few minutes, I'd like to talk about some of the things that I've learned during my career, which I hope will help you follow your dream.

Do what you love

A wise person once said, "If you love what you do, you'll never work a day in your life."

Early in life, I identified what I most loved to do and have been fortunate to be able to make a living doing it. If I could wish one thing for you, professionally speaking, it would be for you to find what you love to do and that you would be able to pursue it professionally.

Always seek excellence

My father was a golf course superintendent. And while he was a great man, we sure weren't rich. So, early on, I knew I had to find a way to earn a living.

And you might not know this, but when I turned pro back in 1954, there certainly wasn't as much prize money as there is today. In fact, it took me 14 years on tour to win as much money as first place pays for some four-day tournaments today. But there was plenty of stiff competition from guys like Gary Player and Jack Nicklaus.

So I knew if I was going to make a living and be successful in my chosen field, I would have to learn as much as I could about my profession, practice those fundamentals every day, and always try to do my best.

I agree with Jim when he says we should seek excellence, not perfection. Seeking perfection is unrealistic and can even be counterproductive. Seeking excellence is not only possible, but it does two very important things: It sets you on a path of high performance that will lead you to extreme levels of professional success and it sets the performance standard for others.

If there is anything about my career that inspires you, I hope it's that when you watch me doing my job you see me seeking excellence. And when others are watching you go about your work, I hope they are also inspired by your own quest for excellence.

Be what you appear to be

One thing that the game of golf teaches is ethical behavior. Jim says his experts on this topic define ethics as "devotion to the unenforceable." That certainly defines the behavior of golfers, because, unlike in many sports, golfers are expected to know the rules and penalize themselves, even when no one is watching.

Over two thousand years ago, Socrates said, "The shortest and surest way to live with honor in the world is to be in reality what you appear to be."

To me, the ethical behavior fostered in the rules of golf, and practiced by those who play it, is one of the most important reasons that the game has endured for so long and is so loved by so many.

In this book, Jim proposes that the color of ethics is gray. What he means is that choices that are black or white are easy. It's the gray areas of life and business that test our character.

Whether you're playing golf or running a business, if you're devoted to the unenforceable, you will be what you appear to be.

Value those who love you

Never underestimate–or undervalue–the power and importance of those who love and support you. Jim says they're the people who care enough about you to simultaneously be your critics and your safe harbors.

I've been blessed with a support group comprised of loving family and friends, and there is no single aspect of my life that has been more critical to my success as a golfer, as a businessman, or as a human being.

Jim tells a story about a turtle that was found on top of a fence post, enjoying his new perspective of the world. Of course, we know that turtle didn't get there by himself. Well, I'm just like that turtle, and I'll bet you are, too.

When your efforts in life or business seem to be missing the fairway too many times, remember that, like the turtle, you've got folks willing help you if you'll let them.

And when an unusually high percentage of your approach shots in life and business are landing near the hole, before you attribute this fortune to your own brilliance, don't forget that you probably had a lot of help reaching such a lofty perch.

I'm particularly honored to be able to contribute to Jim's new book. As a golfer, his swing may not be one to emulate, but when it comes to helping you have, as he says, "the maximum opportunity to be successful," Jim Blasingame has few peers. I recommend a teaching pro to help you with your golf swing, and I recommend Jim Blasingame to help you with your small business.

One of the best ways to accomplish the things I've talked about is to read and apply the success keys Jim provides in *Three Minutes To Success*. Whether you're reading his words or listening to him on his talk show, Jim is truly "the voice of small business."

Finally, as a fellow small business owner, let me say how proud I am of your contribution to the world. Jim's right when he says you're among our modern-day heroes.

Good luck, and may your life and business always be better than par.

Arnold Palmer
Small business owner
and professional golfer

Introduction

One of the things I believe about the 21st century marketplace is that the impact of small businesses will be much more in evidence than it was in the last century.

Want some numbers to back up my claim? Well, the U.S. Small Business Administration reports that small firms currently produce over half of the $11 trillion U.S. gross domestic product. And that same group signs the front of over half of all employee paychecks each week. That sounds pretty significant to me.

Truth is, small businesses have always been important. In fact, it's only been in the last 150 years or so that there was anything but small businesses in the marketplace. Indeed, the original businesses—shopkeepers, bakers, blacksmiths, craftsmen, etc.—were in fact what we now call home-based businesses. And with the increasing number of home-based businesses today, it looks like the marketplace may be coming around full circle.

Every year experts come up with new perspectives on how to operate a business. And while it's good to have different ways of teaching about business, it's also important to realize that the fundamentals of running a business haven't really changed. It's still necessary to work hard, deliver quality goods and services, treat employees and partners with dignity, and of course, take care of the most important members of our businesses, our customers.

Something else that hasn't changed is the laws of economics. Even though during the so-called "Dot Com" era of the 1990s some participants tried to prove otherwise, businesses still have to sell something useful to customers, and make a profit doing it. And as essential as being profitable is for long-term success, cash is still king when it comes to making payroll and keeping the doors open this week.

Now let's talk about what *has* changed.

Although it seems as if we've experienced a lot of change in the past couple of decades, the truth is the only thing different about today from 10 years ago (or 1,000 years ago) is the velocity of change. Most new developments today are really just the next generation of what came before—a computer is just a modern-day wheel or lever—but each new generation is coming faster than the last one. And that increased velocity is what's gotten everyone so excited.

Change has always been an abiding part of life and work. But when our grandparents experienced change, it happened at a pace which allowed them to manage it. Much of the change you and I experience today is happening so fast that it can at once frighten us and give us the impression that we're seeing something new.

In the 21st century there are no new rules, just new tools.

Consequently, my advice to a small business owner today wouldn't be much different if I were writing this 30 years ago:

- Learn and practice the fundamentals of operating a business.

- Anticipate the changes that you can.

- Prepare yourself and your organization to be able to deal with the pace of change, as well as the changes you didn't see coming.

- And don't forget to have fun.

The primary focus of my first book, *Small Business Is Like A Bunch Of Bananas*, was, as I wrote, "... about the human behind the entrepreneurial dream; the one facing the challenges of operating a small business; the person with the bull's eye on top of the head where the proverbial 'buck' keeps stopping."

This first book is primarily devoted to the operating fundamentals of running a successful business. But since I think small business success is impossible without performing regular maintenance on the spirit of the owner, about 20% of this book —every fifth or sixth chapter—addresses that element of success. Frankly, it's doubtful that you will ever read anything by me that doesn't deal, at least in part, with the human side of being a small business owner.

Topics we'll cover in this book include profitability, branding, capitalization, and how to be a successful employer. You'll also find keys to managing the financial part of your business, as well as the human side.

Being a business owner is like being a parent: It doesn't require genius, or even much talent, just to be one. But being a successful one, well that's different.

Woody Allen once said that 80% of life is just showing up. I think that also applies to business success. The other 20% is focusing on the fundamentals.

Jim Blasingame
The Small Business Advocate

How to use this book

Three minutes to success. That's a pretty bold statement, isn't it. *Who does this guy Blasingame think he is, anyway?*

If that's what you're thinking, fair enough.

It's true. You can't be a success in just three minutes. Maybe not even in three years.

But if you're trying to understand the fundamentals of starting, running, and growing a small business, wouldn't it help if you had many of those fundamentals presented to you in a handy package, where the information cuts to the chase?

And what if that same package introduced you to those fundamentals not only in such a way that you now know they exist, but also helps you realize that you need to know more? Isn't it just possible that such a handy package could put you on the road to success?

Well, okay, then.

Three Minutes to Success is composed of 52 classic small business lessons. Why 52? Well, it occurred to me that you might want to focus on a different topic each week. Of course, you can also look in the Table of Contents for the topic that's on your mind. And by the way, I don't just preach adding value, I practice it. This book actually has two bonus chapters. You're welcome.

As mentioned, and as you will see, this book is not intended as a textbook that covers all aspects of a topic. Rather, its purpose is to introduce you to many of the fundamentals of operating a business, which I hope will encourage you to take the next step to learn more.

As you're reading, if you already know about a particular business fundamental, congratulations. You've just been reminded. If you didn't know about it, congratulations. You've just been introduced.

The best way to describe the style of this book is short and sweet—maximum message, minimum words. To support this style, each subject has been written so that the chapters are no more than two pages long.

In case you don't already know this, I'm kind of a contrarian. It's one of my many charming and endearing characteristics. For example, most books begin each chapter on the right-hand page. The architecture of this book has each two-page chapter beginning on the left-hand page, so you can keep the whole subject in front of you without turning the page.

I like what architects say about this kind of thinking: "Form follows function."

At the end of each chapter, you'll find my patented signature, "Write this on a rock ..." Those who know me well think this is a reference to the density of my skull. But as you'll see, it's the essence of what has been said in each chapter.

So, now you're set. I hope you enjoy our time together, and that something I say will motivate you to focus on the fundamentals just a little more, so you can have the maximum opportunity to be successful.

Now, let the reading, the execution and the success begin. And let's have some fun, too.

Three Minutes to Success

*52 classic small business lessons
you can read in 3 minutes*

Myths of business ownership

As the fertility of entrepreneurial soil improves in the 21st century, your chances of meeting a starry-eyed human being, babbling on about the prospect of becoming a business owner, will also improve.

Probing for the object of this person's entrepreneurial infatuation will precipitate the what, where, how and when questions, and ultimately the most important one: *Why* do you want to own a business?

Answers to this question, unfortunately, often produce what I call "The Myths of Small Business Ownership." Here are four:

Myth 1: *When I'm an owner, I'll be my own boss.*

That's right; you won't have an employer telling you what to do. But you'll trade that one boss for many others: customers, landlords, bankers, the IRS, regulators, even employees.

In today's marketplace, there is less "bossing" and more leading, managing and partnering. In a small business, everyone must wear several hats and the dominator management model doesn't work well in this multi-tasking environment.

Myth 2: *When I own my own business, I won't have to work as hard as I do now.*

This is actually true—you will work much harder. Ramona Arnett, CEO of Ramona Enterprises, said it best: "Owning a business is when you work 80 hours a week so you can avoid working 40 hours for someone else."

The irony is you will actually *want* to work harder when you understand that everything in your business belongs to you, even the irritating, frustrating and frightening challenges of ownership. These will take on a new perspective when you realize that you also own the *opportunities* you turn those challenges into.

You'll turn the lights on in the morning and off in the evening not because you want to work more, but because you won't want to miss any part of your dream coming true.

Myth 3: *When I own my own business, I can take a day off whenever I want.*

Well, maybe. You may find that your business has such a compelling attraction that you won't want to take off as much as you might think.

If you love to play golf, you may actually play less as an owner than you did as an employee. Not because you no longer love golf, but because the love of your business might exceed that of golf.

Whatever interests you had as an employee will likely become jealous of your business.

Why do you want to own a business?

Myth 4: *When I own my own business, I'll make a lot of money.*

If the only reason you want to own a business is to get rich, you probably won't be a happy owner. Brace yourself: The National Federation of Independent Business (NFIB) says the average annual income of small business owners in America is about $40,000.

You actually could get rich, but it's more likely that you'll just make a living.

Being a successful owner first means loving what you do. Pursuing wealth should be secondary, and ironically, is more likely to happen when in this subordinate role.

Write this on a rock ... For maximum small business success, dispel the myths of ownership.

Three management best practices

Business Planning

If you don't know where you're going, any road will take you there.

This is an old adage, but one we should all post on our office walls. Clearly, the best road for a small business to take is the one built in a written business plan.

Yeah, I know, you've got your plan in your head. But there's one big problem with that strategy: You're the only one who has access to it.

Business plans need to be available to managers, advisors, bankers, and sometimes investors, which requires words and numbers—on paper.

Here's an excellent reason to have a written business plan: It's the best medicine to prevent the toxic practice called "crisis management." By regularly comparing your plan to actual performance, a problem that might have become organizational double pneumonia turns into a management sneeze that you take in stride.

In the beginning you'll have to show the discipline and courage to deal with the crisis-of-the-hour while you're executing your plan. But soon you'll see how both the size and frequency of crises will diminish.

And every day you execute your plan, while polishing off leftover crises, is a day closer to the opposite of crisis management—successful management.

Leadership

The two most consistent characteristics found in successful business owners are leadership and the ability to foster leadership in others.

Five things we know about leaders:
1. Leaders are consistent in their behavior.
2. Leaders can be trusted to do what they say and deliver what they promise.
3. Leaders know that the success of others is important.
4. Leaders are courageous.
5. Leaders find people who will follow them.

Some people seem to be natural leaders, but nothing they do is anything the rest of us can't learn.

Leveraging intellectual property (IP)

A recent survey showed that in 1978, 80% of a corporation's assets were tangible, such as equipment and inventory, while the rest were intellectual assets, like software, patents, etc. But by 1997, the ratio of tangible to intellectual assets had essentially reversed, with 73% of corporate assets being in IP.

This survey focused on large corporations, but the IP trend certainly applies equally to small firms. The only difference is that big companies have always valued their IP, regardless of its percentage of total assets, while small companies typically have not.

"If you don't know where you're going, any road will take you there."

In the 21st century, small businesses must start identifying and valuing IP, so we can more fully leverage the power of these assets.

Write this on a rock ... You don't have to be Super Manager. Just focus on the fundamentals and best management practices.

Building a community

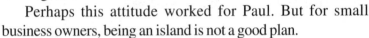

I am a rock, I am an i-i-island.

These are the title lyrics of a 1967 Simon and Garfunkel song. Paul Simon wrote it while he was "finding himself" in London.

Perhaps this attitude worked for Paul. But for small business owners, being an island is not a good plan.

So how do you make sure you don't become an island? Build a community—preferably, several communities.

Webster says a community is "a unified body of individuals." Let's take that definition to the next level by making it possessive, as in, "*your* community."

Not your geographic community. Rather, the community of people who know, support, and depend on you, *wherever* they may be. And here's the pivotal point to understand: In your community, as Webster might define the term, you are the unifying force.

There is great power in recognizing the unifying influence you have on your community, especially when you exercise that influence for the benefit of all the members, including yourself.

Success and community

It's important and productive to think about the power of community as leverage in your effort to carve out a niche in the marketplace. Being able to create and unify a community that's available to you—and you to it—is essential to small business success.

Dave Longaberger, a learning-disabled stutterer who turned his father's basket-weaving hobby into a billion-dollar-a-year business, said it this way: "Your success will ultimately depend on the relationships you build." Community.

So, how do you build your community? One word:

networking. In *Masters Of Networking*, Ivan Misner, founder of Business Network International wrote: "The most successful people surround themselves with a well-developed, sophisticated support network." Community.

Chicken or egg?

There is no mystery here: The egg—networking—definitely comes first, followed by the chicken—community. Networking without an awareness of, and a goal toward, building communities is like what Texans call an urban cowboy: all hat and no cattle. If you're networking without unifying those contacts into communities, you're wasting a lot of people's time, including your own.

Being able to create and unify a community is essential to small business success.

Networking done well produces many different kinds of communities: business communities, friendship communities, avocational communities, etc. And in the 21st century, it's important to realize that your communities include people you have met, plus those who are part of your virtual communities.

Building, unifying, and influencing communities is a proven way to be successful, and an excellent way to create happiness for all of the members of your communities.

Write this on a rock ... Master carpenters build houses. Master networkers build communities. Get off of your island and start building.

Reinvention or extinction

If you're a small business owner, there is an excellent chance that you've reinvented yourself at least once in your life. There was probably a moment, an inspiration, an event, a conversation, a pink slip, etc., that caused you to start that new journey.

It's also a safe bet that you've discovered you must keep reinventing your business, too. And this reinvention process can never stop, because every day the marketplace becomes less like a station and more like a moving train.

Indeed, the Hobson's choice for small businesses is reinvention or extinction.

Reinventing your business

In his book, *Creative Approaches For The Cost Effective Organization*, Steve Martin says there are five generations of corporate growth:

1. Work. The entrepreneurial stage.
2. Sell. Focus on sales growth and market share.
3. Cut. Focus on efficiencies to drive the bottom line.
4. Buy. Acquire assets to reach the next level.
5. Think. All actions are proactive, as intellectual and financial resources focus on *knowing* the next best step instead of guessing.

It's almost a natural law that a successful business will reinvent itself along these five generational lines.

Synchronized reinvention

While you're reinventing your business, be sure to do the same for yourself, because each generation of a company's growth requires a different kind of manager. And while you're making sure that your personal growth isn't behind your company's progress, don't get too far ahead, either.

Unfortunately, there is no corresponding natural law to help keep your personal reinvention matched up with, and parallel to, that of your company. Consequently, keeping your personal intellectual growth in sync with your business requires constant attention and honest self-analysis.

Reinventing yourself

Personal reinvention doesn't mean you go from being a surveyor to being a surgeon. It means that instead of being intimidated by technological advancements, you actually become a visionary expert on how to leverage new capability.

It means you go from knowing nothing about how an earthquake or a military *coup d'etat* on the other side of the planet could affect your business six months from now, to being pretty good at identifying local as well as global threats and opportunities.

While you're reinventing your business, be sure to do the same for yourself.

Perhaps the best example is when you're able to delegate tasks to the capable staff you've hired that you once trusted only yourself to do.

Embrace change

Sometimes circumstances require you to reinvent yourself whether you're ready or not. When that happens, you can choose to be a whiny victim or embrace the change. But remember this: Only owners who embrace change can run and grow successful businesses.

Write this on a rock ... Reinvention or extinction—the choice is yours.

The small business gift

George was an unlikely success story, and certainly no hero. Reluctantly drawn into the family small business, year after year he went about all the duties of an owner, from manager to visionary. And he experienced all of the realities of ownership, including the occasional brief indulgence in self-satisfaction, as well as the deferred gratification that is usually heavy on the deferred part.

In his own eyes, George never quite measured up. His best friend left their small town and went off to make a fortune and travel the world. His brother went off to war and became a national hero. George stayed home in boring Small Town, America and minded the family store.

At a particularly low point in George's life, when it seemed all was lost, our small business owner did more than contemplate suicide—he stepped right up on its dark threshold and looked inside that abyss.

What created this sad scenario that threatened to put George over the edge? He was visited by one of the usual culprits that cast their shadows over so many small business owners, like a ghost of decisions past. It was something about finances, and George wished he had never been born.

But before he could carry out his act of desperation, George was given a gift. He was shown how the world would look if he had never lived. It wasn't pretty.

Yes, it's that George

By now I'm sure you are getting ahead of me. You no doubt recognize our friend as George Bailey, the owner of The Building and Loan in the Frank Capra classic, "It's a Wonderful Life." I've seen that movie at least a hundred times and never get tired of it. (But even though it's critical to the plot, I still can't watch the part where Uncle Billy loses the $8,000.)

The reason I'm retelling this story here is because everything said previously—right up to the part about the gift—could be about you and me. To be sure, small business ownership has many advantages, and can be extremely fulfilling. But it can also be lonely, frightening, and frequented by ghosts of decisions past. And sometimes, like George, we feel that we just don't measure up.

Here's your gift

Remember George's angel, Clarence ASC (Angel Second Class)? Well, let me be your angel, and here's your gift: You make a difference to your family, your employees and their families, your customers and their families, your community, your marketplace, your nation, and this planet. Without you, small business owner, the world would be like Bedford Falls without George Bailey—not a pretty picture.

Small business ownership has many advantages, and can be extremely fulfilling.

Next time you are visited by a ghost of decisions past or some other setback, dwell on it long enough to take corrective action. But never forget to take stock of all the important things that you do for so many.

I may be the only one who tells you this every day, but you're not just my hero, you're a hero to a lot of people. And I don't want to see what the world would look like without all the good that you do.

Write this on a rock ... The spirit of small business—your spirit—is a wonderful gift to the world.

Getting a bank loan: Part 1

Do you know how a bank makes a decision to loan (or not loan) you money for your business? If your answer is no, don't ask a bank for a loan yet, because you're not ready. You have homework to do.

But don't worry, it's not that complicated. You may already know more than you think, because getting a bank loan is a lot like qualifying a prospective customer. For example, you want to know the following three things (we'll cover three more in the next chapter):

1. Who makes the decision?
2. What do they need?
3. How do they want your information?

Just like in selling, part of the qualifying process is to do your homework. Here's how this works with banks:

Who makes the decision?

You have the right to ask who is going to make the decision on your loan. Can your loan officer make the loan, or will it have to go to the loan committee, or out of town?

Why do you care? The more people involved in the process, the greater the scrutiny of your deal, which means more questions and more time from proposal to answer.

You might be able to get this information by just paying attention. If not, ask, because you need to know:

- How many proposal packages to prepare.
- How long it should take to get an answer.
- How to prepare for any questions your loan officer didn't ask.
- How important it may be to take your proposal to more than one bank.

What do they need?

Your banker will ask for personal and business financial statements. They might accept last year's business numbers, but they could also ask for interim numbers.

Depending on the size of your request and what you're using the money for, your banker might ask for your business plan. If you want to buy equipment or a vehicle that can be used as collateral, your plan may not be necessary, but have it ready. If the loan is to buy real estate, you'll need a current appraisal.

Don't give them more than they ask for, or before they ask for it. But the quicker you can give them what they want, the quicker you'll get an answer.

The more you know about what could be requested, the

Getting a bank loan is a lot like qualifying a prospective customer.

better prepared you'll be, and the more professional—and credit worthy—you'll appear.

How do they want your info?

Ask your banker how he or she would like to see your information and proposal: verbally, in writing, a PowerPoint presentation? Find out how they want it and give it to them— as soon as possible.

Whether you're borrowing $5,000 for a computer, or $5 million to buy out a competitor, learn as much as you can about what's going on inside the paneled walls of your bank while you're waiting for an answer.

Write this on a rock ... Qualify a bank like you do customers, and be sure to do your homework.

Getting a bank loan: Part 2

In the previous chapter we talked about three things you need to know to qualify a bank so you can get a business loan. Here are three more things you need to find out:

1. What motivates them?
2. How motivated are they?
3. What do you have to do?

What motivates them?

All banks need to make loans, but all banks don't like the same kinds of loans.

Some banks are set up to make working capital loans, and some aren't. Most banks make real estate loans, but each one has its own profile of what kind of real estate they will consider. And all banks like to loan money for things with serial numbers, like vehicles and equipment.

In your meetings, what your banker says about your proposal should indicate his or her level of interest in your type of loan. But if not, it's okay to ask.

Banks will fight for loans, but they'll kill for deposits. Checking account deposits are virtually free money to a bank, a portion of which they use to make loans. They like personal checking accounts, but they *love* business accounts.

A bank's motivation could increase if you have daily deposits of any size and are willing to place your operating account with them. You should know the value of your deposits to a bank, and use that information to your advantage.

How motivated are they?

Typically, you can tell how motivated a bank is by how helpful the loan officer is. Her excitement is no foreteller of success, just of motivation. But if she seems indifferent or unmotivated, that's probably not a good sign.

A deal that couldn't get through the front door of Bank A this morning could be received with a red carpet at Bank B this afternoon. So you might want to take your proposal to more than one bank.

Don't wait until you've been turned down by one bank to take your proposal to a second one.

What do I have to do?

Bankers love field trips. Give your bankers a demonstration of the new equipment the loan is for, or take them to see the building or land you want to buy.

Banks will fight for loans, but they'll kill for deposits.

Be sure to show them how the object of your loan request will help you grow your business, profits and deposits.

The best way to get a business loan is to do your homework, anticipate what your banker needs, and get them what they ask for.

And if the bank that was loyal to you when you needed it doesn't have the best deal—but it's a deal you can live with—"dance with the one that brung you."

Write this on a rock ... Getting a bank loan is like qualifying a prospective customer. Performing this process will significantly improve your chances of getting a loan.

Seeking Investors

Small business capital comes from three primary sources:
1. Profits left in the business
2. Debt, like a bank loan
3. Equity investment.

The challenge is to blend the right amount from each source into your capitalization plan.

In recent years, acceptance of the third source, investor capital, has increased among small business owners as well as investors. And while many elements of finding and acquiring investor capital are similar to getting a bank loan, the investor process is much longer and much more complex.

In his book, *Raising Capital*, my friend, Andrew Sherman lists several common mistakes entrepreneurs make searching for investment capital. Below are six of Andrew's "mistakes," each followed by my thoughts:

Mistake: *Using an investor search that's too broad.*

Each investment firm has a strategy that fits its interest. An investor who likes medical ventures won't be a prospect for your retail franchise idea.

Qualifying each investor prospect before making contact will greatly improve your search efficiency.

Mistake: *Misjudging the time involved.*

Part of Murphy's Law states that everything will take longer than you think.

Alas, Mr. Murphy is alive and well in the investment market-place. It usually takes months, not weeks, to find, approach and get an answer from investors. And remember, like prayers, the answer may be "no."

Mistake: *Falling in love with your business plan.*

Every mother's baby is beautiful, but your plan is not your investor prospect's baby.

Accept that your business plan will likely have to be adjusted before you get funded. So be prepared to accept capital that's tied to modifications to your plan.

Mistake: *Taking your financial projections too seriously.*

First let's establish the prime rule of investment evaluation: All projections are wrong!

Of course, you can show projections you believe are achievable. But also include a set that shows at least where your break-even point is if things don't go so well.

Accept that your business plan will likely have to be adjusted.

Mistake: *Confusing product development with sales development.*

Investors love real customers and real sales. Nevertheless, even projections based on history will be highly scrutinized. But sales projections based on projected products will be highly doubted.

Mistake: *Failing to recognize the importance of the management team.*

A good management team can fix a bad plan, but a bad team can ruin a good plan. Unless you're asking investors to also contribute management expertise, which is not unusual, don't seek investor capital without a qualified management team.

Write this on a rock ... The most valuable lessons are learned from mistakes. Make your own, not these.

Speak the language

Once upon a time, a storm caused two ships to sink in the same area. All on board were lost at sea, save one from each ship, and those poor souls were alive only because they swam to a small island nearby.

As luck would have it, the two men hauled themselves up on the beach at the same time and within sight of each other. But the survivors' celebration soon became pensive as they realized that each spoke a language unknown to the other.

Immediately, both men had the same unspoken thought: "I don't know this man or the language he speaks, but if we're going to survive, we have to find a way to communicate and work together."

Real world castaways

In many ways, this tale actually plays out every day.

But instead of on the high seas, our story takes place in the marketplace. And instead of mythical shipwreck survivors, our real life players are small business owners and bankers.

Like the castaways in the first story, the excitement of the latter two about their future prospects turns pensive when they both realize that: 1) They need each other in order to be successful; and 2) they don't speak each other's language very well, if at all.

With so much common interest and so little mutual understanding, can these two create a successful survival story? Absolutely, but only if they have the:

**Blasingame Official Translator
for Bankers and Small Business Owners**

Here are a few examples of how The Translator works:

Small business owners speaking "banker"

1. Identify your banker as a success partner and your business's best friend.

2. Stay close to your banker when things are going well, and even closer when things aren't going so well.

3. Believe that an uninformed banker is a scared banker, and a scared banker cannot, and will not, behave like a partner.

4. Pay attention to what motivates and impresses a banker, like attention to detail.

5. Understand pertinent bank rules and regulations, so as not to ask for something that can't be done.

6. Reward banker loyalty with small business loyalty.

Bankers speaking "small business"

1. Understand that all small businesses are undercapitalized.

2. Recognize that starting a small business is easy—operating a successful one is not.

3. Explain bank rules and banking regulations more often.

4. Realize that it's the banker's job to recommend services and products first.

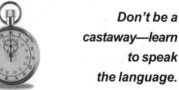

Don't be a castaway—learn to speak the language.

5. Believe that small businesses need more than loans and financial services—they need technical assistance from their partners, like explaining how a business can grow itself right *out* of business.

6. In the credit scoring process, always find a way to give small business owners credit for character and best efforts.

7. Reward small business loyalty with banker loyalty.

Write this on a rock ... For small businesses and banks to avoid being 21st century castaways, they must speak each other's language and become partners.

Lessons from the farm

Growing up on a farm provided many valuable lessons that have transferred beautifully to my life in the non-farming marketplace.

Here are three of those timeless lessons.

Ten pigs to the litter

Deciding to raise feeder pigs, a young farmer based his financial projections on two well-known facts: 1) A sow can give birth to a litter of 10 piglets or more; and 2) it's possible for a sow to deliver three litters in one year.

Using these two as assumptions, plus the number of his sows and the market price of pigs, this rural entrepreneur eagerly forecasted potential revenue. The product of this equation gave him visions of being in Hog Heaven.

But the young farmer would soon become acquainted with two other facts: Assumptions are often wrong, and projections are always wrong.

Forecasting is an important business planning tool, but the road to bankruptcy is paved with the equity of those who did too much multiplying and not enough discounting.

Plan for success, but beware the folly of forecasting "10 pigs to the litter."

The china egg

"Farm-fresh eggs." Seeing those words on a breakfast menu harkens me back to when that was a daily reality.

But farmers know hens don't lay eggs so we can have breakfast. Consequently, they harvest the fresh eggs each day, and leave a china egg in each nest, which is sufficient to prevent the hens from abandoning their nests and continue production.

There are china eggs in business, too. They're the prospects you keep calling on who never buy anything.

Since you're smarter than a chicken, don't spend time and resources sitting on china eggs.

On the farm or in business, china eggs never hatch.

Half of your herd

A young cattleman was in the process of buying his first bull. Inspecting the offerings at a sale, the lad struck up a conversation with an elderly gent.

"Think I'll save some money and buy one of the cheaper bulls," the whippersnapper said, trying in vain to sound smarter than he was.

With great gentleness, the old man responded with, "A good bull is 50% of your herd."

As the greenhorn nodded, acting like he already knew that,

Assumptions are often wrong, and projections are always wrong.

this Yoda-in-overalls hit the young pup with the other half of his maxim: "But a bad bull is 100% of your herd."

If you're in the delivery business, maintain a good fleet even if you have to eat bologna. If you're a software developer, make sure you have the best technology available, even if you have to drive an old car.

Small businesses always have great needs but limited resources. The challenge is in effectively and strategically deploying those resources.

Good tools are 50% of what you accomplish in business; bad tools —100%.

Write this on a rock ... City folk shouldn't look down their noses at their country cousins. Before there were cities, farmers were learning and sharing many important lessons for life and business.

Small business characters

Once, a friend of mine was sacked.

No, the Huns didn't do it—one of the Baby Bells did. But they called it "downsizing." And as millions of us have, upon being sacked he decided to start his own small business.

I remember those days. You don't know whether the rush you're feeling is excitement about the possibility of success, or stark terror about the possibility of failure. The truth is, it's a little of both.

The Chinese word for crisis is written with two characters: the first signifying danger and the second, opportunity. Leave it to the Chinese to deliver maximum message with minimum words.

I don't know what the Chinese word for entrepreneur looks like, but if they ask my opinion I will tell them to wrap danger and opportunity around the characters that stand for vision, courage, and energy. Let me explain.

Danger

Danger is an abiding element in the world of entrepreneurs. I believe you can't have the latter without the former. Sometimes entrepreneurship is created by danger. My friend lost his job, and the danger of being unemployed caused him to consider taking entrepreneurial action. If necessity is the mother of invention, danger may be its grandmother.

Vision

For entrepreneurs, vision is the zoom lens of our desire. Some spark of necessity, fear, or creativity causes us to fix our focus on a particular subject and gradually bring it into closer and clearer view.

Zooming in, our perspective will change with information acquired at each focal length. Along the way, we make adjustments to our plan for the object of our entrepreneurial affection—our business. And since vision is personal, it's also limitless.

Courage

As you deploy your vision, opportunities for action will present themselves, putting courage front and center.

Entrepreneurship without courage is like religion without faith. If you're frustrated because your plans aren't coming together, look inside yourself. You may not have the courage to risk the danger inherent in being an entrepreneur. If that's the case, you may be one of the most valuable forces in the market-place—an employee with vision.

If necessity is the mother of invention, danger may be its grandmother.

Energy

I know lots of entrepreneurs, but I don't know any success-ful ones who are lazy. There's just something about working without a net that gets your energy pumping.

Entrepreneurial energy may be the most powerful force in the marketplace. If you have it, use it wisely. If you are an observer of it, the awe you feel is justified.

Opportunity

Finally, the other bookend character and the Holy Grail of entrepreneurs—opportunity. In terms of entrepreneurial motiva-tion, if danger is the stick, opportunity is the carrot.

Write this on a rock ... You don't have to know Chinese to be a successful small business owner, but you do need to understand the characters of an entrepreneur.

Your thoughts

_____

_____

_____

_____

_____

_____

_____

_____

_____

_____

_____

_____

_____

_____

_____

_____

_____

Two key marketplace relationships

Of the thousands of words in the English language, there are a few that are particularly powerful; not because of how they sound, but because of what they stand for. One of my favorites is *marketplace*.

The marketplace is as close to a living, breathing organism as any non-sentient entity could be. When you say or write marketplace, you evoke a sense of energy, vitality, dynamism, productivity, and cooperation.

But as powerfully positive as this description sounds, the marketplace is actually cruelly indifferent to our very existence, let alone whether we succeed or fail. It is at once a place of opportunity and failure, and whichever we find depends more on us than anything or anyone else.

The divining rod of success in the marketplace will always twitch in the direction of our first topic: being customer focused.

It's all about them

A customer's relationship with your business is as simple as it is rude—it's all about them. And the sooner you accept this truth, the sooner people will line up to come into your business.

Unfortunately, this truth isn't intuitive because of the process used to develop your products and services. In that process, you're the customer buying benefits for your business. But benefits to you morph into mere features when presented to your customers. And as we know, customers buy benefits, not features.

Success may be waiting on you to make the conversion from being excited about your stuff to getting your *customers* excited about your stuff.

WIIFM: What's In It For Me? That's what customers are asking, and you must be able to provide the answer.

Find vendor partners

Now let's discuss vendor relationships.

In the 21st century, these are really strategic alliances, because a vendor's success depends on your ability to acquire and serve customers with what you buy from them.

To gain and maintain a competitive advantage, talk with vendors to see what they can offer your alliance in addition to just their stuff. They may already

Customers buy benefits, not features.

have a plan you can participate in. If not, identify what it will take to increase sales or improve service, and ask them to participate.

Examples might be co-op advertising, or joint calls with your customers to introduce a new product or provide technical assistance in a customer application. Or there might be an opportunity for the vendor to provide consignment inventory to help you expand your lines, if you're currently unable to capitalize new ones on your own.

Remember, your relationship with vendors should be as much a partnership as a business deal. If you don't find an attitude of partnership with any vendor, find another vendor.

Like busses, there'll be another one along in six minutes.

Write this on a rock ... Marketplace Rule #1: Focus on the customer. Marketplace Rule #2: see Rule #1.

Become a partner

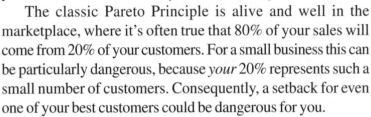

Do you know what wakes your customers up in the middle of the night?

Why is this important? Because the challenges of your customers will eventually roll downhill to you.

The classic Pareto Principle is alive and well in the marketplace, where it's often true that 80% of your sales will come from 20% of your customers. For a small business this can be particularly dangerous, because *your* 20% represents such a small number of customers. Consequently, a setback for even one of your best customers could be dangerous for you.

While inevitable, these events don't have to be surprises. If you pay attention to what's happening in your customers' industries and the marketplace, you'll be better prepared to help them, which obviously helps you.

Prepare to move fast

You should be reading the trade journals your best customers are reading, which have news and trends about their industry. Another way to find out what's going on is to ask.

Ask customers how their business is doing. Talk about the global issues and influences in their industry. Don't worry; customers like it when you show an interest in them.

In the 21st century, when a challenge or opportunity causes a customer to make fast adjustments, they will only take their fastest vendors with them. Make sure that's you.

Read, ask, listen and learn. Then respond with a market strategy that helps customers with their challenges. It's the straightest line to customer loyalty and consistent success.

Be integrated and indispensable

Knowing what worries customers segues perfectly to our next

topic: Become indispensable by being integrated.

Small businesses are playing a more integrated role in the 21st century operations of their larger customers.

If you're merely a vendor, you're like that one-every-six-minutes bus we've talked about. But when you're integrated into a customer's operation, you become as important as an internal division. For example:

Instead of just delivering your products to the customer's loading dock, how would their operating efficiencies improve if you took the goods all the way to the end-user?

The challenges of your customers will eventually roll downhill to you.

Create your own ideas by turning the way you do business with your customers upside-down and see if any integration opportunities fall out.

How much should you charge for this level of service? Ask your customer how much it would be worth. But don't forget to discount it by how much becoming integrated and indispensable is worth to you.

Opportunities abound for those who see integration possibilities and can think like a big business while delivering the efficiencies, versatility and nimbleness of a small business.

Write this on a rock ... Your customers' world is evolving, and moving fast. How closely is your business tracking with it?

Waking up in Wal-World

Riinngg—Riinngg—Ri...

"Uh, hallow."

"Good morning, Walter, this is your wake-up call. It's 6:30 a.m. in Wal-World, time zone 3, Wednesday, April 21, 2075. Current temperature is a crisp 11 degrees Wal-Cius. Have a nice day."

Walter Wallace had received the same phone call every morning of his life since he was eight years old. That was 2048, the year planet Earth, as he and all other Earthlings had known it for thousands of years, became Wal-World, wholly-owned by Wal-Mart.

In the 50 years prior to 2048, the world economy gradually became dominated by Wal-Mart. By 2030, the company had moved its headquarters from Arkansas to occupy the entire lower third of the island formerly known as Manhattan—now called New Wal-Town. From its offices on Wal-Street, the company quite literally changed the world.

Walking to his job as a Wal-Mart community planner later that morning, Walter stopped at a Wal-Mac kiosk to get breakfast. As he swiped his Wal-Card to pay, a strange noise began coming out of the machine.

Eeep-Eeep-Ee -

"Wazzat?" Walter grunted, as he slapped the snooze button. "Where am I?"

"Honey, are you okay?" Walter's wife, Wilma asked. "You've had a nightmare."

"Boy, I'll say," Walter sighed, wiping the sweat from the back of his neck. "I dreamed Wal-Mart had taken over the world. I tell you, Wilma, it was awful—they owned everything. There were no small businesses anywhere."

Opening the morning paper later at breakfast, Walter felt a

chill as he read this very real headline:

*WAL-MART BECOMES WORLD'S
LARGEST CORPORATION!*

A war you can win

In his small business later that day, Walter thought about his nightmare, the newspaper headline, and another dream of his— the one about passing his small business to his children.

Meeting with his employees, Walter vowed to fight the Big Boxes the only way a small business can. "The price war is over and we lost," he declared. "And we may not be able to win the selection war, either. But we can win the service, innovation, and creativity war.

"We must focus only on those customers who want value, not just price. Our value proposition must be driven by *how* our customers want what we sell, *when* they want it, and *where* they want it delivered. Not the price tag!

> *We can win the service, innovation, and creativity war.*

"We have to convince our targeted customers that, when customization matters, when technical support matters, when their *time* matters, we're the brand of choice.

"And here's the good news: As a small business, we can do all those things better than any Big Box ever did."

Then Walter said, "But if we don't deliver what we promise, we might as well go ahead and move into a Wal-Mart."

Write this on a rock ... Be sure to focus on the growing number of value-conscious customers who appreciate the essence of your small business. And then thank Wal-Mart for keeping everybody else out of your way.

A golden opportunity

Prior to 1975, consumers enjoyed what I call The Golden Age of Customer Service.

Sadly, based on 21ˢᵗ century research, we now appear to be in The Plastic Age of Customer Service.

In the newest American Customer Satisfaction Index, the average customer satisfaction rating was only 57%.

Going six for 10 is pretty good — if you're playing baseball. But during The Golden Age of Customer Service, any business with that batting average was headed for failure.

The plastic triplets

So how has such a level of unservice become a 21ˢᵗ century norm? Because consumers have become sensitized to what I call the Plastic Triplets: high volume, low price, and poor service.

For small businesses, the Plastic Triplets create both opportunity and danger. But seizing the former and avoiding the latter requires an understanding of two things:

1. *Rarely do the high volume, low price siblings appear without bringing along their triplet, poor service.*

Don't get me wrong; there's nothing inherently wrong with high volume. But it becomes bad for small businesses when they join a price war.

And low price is also not inherently bad—for consumers. But it's bad for a small business that turns down that dark and dangerous road.

Remember, the price war is over and small business lost.

2. *Nothing that has happened in the past 30 years has changed how humans want to be treated, only how they expect to be treated.*

Armed with this knowledge and understanding, all a small

business has to do to prove that it isn't plastic is to reverse the order of the Plastic Triplets and rename them.

The golden triplets

Our first new triplet is *excellent service*, which is delivering goods and services in a way that is not only reliable, but also creative and innovative.

The first thing you'll notice is that your customers will be astonished, because remember: humans still want to be treated well, they're just not used to it.

The second new triplet is the mother's milk of small business — *premium prices that deliver high margins*. If you're not charging for the value you deliver, that means you've joined a price war, and you know what we've said about price wars.

The new third triplet is *targeted volume*. As a small business, you not only don't want to do business with everyone, you can't. Target only those customers who want more from you than just price.

The price war is over and small business lost.

The customers you're after want customization, dependability, technical assistance, and one more thing: They want you to save them *time*.

This may be the most important 21st century development on which small businesses must focus: *More and more people are valuing their time more than their money.*

It has been said that the way to a man's heart is through his stomach. But the way to the heart of a 21st century small business customer is through excellent service.

Write this on a rock ... Focus on the Golden Triplets and you'll create your own Golden Age of Customer Service, and outrageous success.

Branding and The Q

Have you noticed that every new on-air person hired by a TV network looks like an actor on a soap opera? They're all young and pretty—even the men.

We're left to think that non-beautiful people don't apply for these positions. That is, unless you're familiar with a certain marketing measurement.

The Q

Marketing Evaluations, Inc. is the proprietor of a marketing metric that's used extensively to hire on-air talent. It's called the Q Score and, as Daniel Henninger wrote in his *Wall Street Journal* column, "It's brutally uncomplicated."

Henninger explains that prospective anchorpeople are presented to an audience who are asked to give one of two answers: "I like," or "I don't like." Responses are graded based on the numeric Q Score. Above 19 means you've "got Q."

Never mind credentials. Henninger says if an applicant "can read large type and has Q, he gets the job." Below 19— fuggedaboutit.

Henninger proposes that the Q Score is "arguably the secret of the universe." He means the universe most modern humans live in, which is "whatever we see on television."

The brand myth

Could the Q factor be involved in perpetuating the market-place myth that owning a brand is the exclusive domain of big business?

After all, it would seem that only the young and beautiful possess the best TV journalism credentials. Why wouldn't we think that a brand is what you get with a glitzy, world-class television promotion?

And since most of us would be guilty of giving an "I like" score to a pretty face, it follows that we would also not think that a dowdy small business could actually own a real brand.

But here's the truth about branding, and it's good news for small business: Owning a brand is more than having Q.

Most experts will testify that a brand is established when a product delivers a desirable feeling. Pleasure, happiness, security, and yes, even pretty, are a few examples of how a brand might make us feel.

Forget eyeballs. True brand value is established when a brand consistently delivers on one or more of our feelings, and pops into our mind's eye the next time we need it.

If people were influenced only by things that have Q, churchgoers would only attend big, beautiful churches. And yet, tiny churches abound.

Like religion, brand loyalty is also a very personal thing. Which is more good news for small business, because getting close enough to customers to know

Owning a brand is more than having Q.

how they want to feel is what a small business does better than any big business.

So it's resolved: Owning a brand is not the exclusive domain of big business. And when it comes to actually building brand value, small businesses have the edge.

Our challenge is in believing this truth, and learning how to dominate with our brands.

Write this on a rock ... Big businesses may be good at brand Q, but small businesses are better at what really counts: building brand value.

Find your spirit

Do you think much about your spirit? You know
—the force that drives your protoplasm around. It's
the keeper of your courage, wisdom, and humanity,
and the only thing that's different about identical twins.

We should all be conscious of our spirit, but for small
business owners, it's essential. Because whether we realize it or
not, as entrepreneurs, our spirit is the part of us that we must be
able to depend upon.

In *Eternal Echoes*, my friend, John O'Donohue, wrote a
passage about the human spirit that certainly speaks to this entrepreneur: "When you open your heart to discovery, you will be
called to step outside the comfort barriers within which you
have fortified your life. You will be called to risk old views and
thoughts ... but your spirit loves the danger of growth."

Discovery

Small business owners "open their hearts to discovery"
every day. Sometimes we discover that our vision, hard work,
and planning have produced a contract with a new customer, a
little more profit on the bottom line, and that we just might make
it another year.

But sometimes our discoveries are not so pleasant—like an
employee who doesn't show up, an expensive equipment breakdown, or a missed bid.

Challenging discoveries are no respecter of businesses, large
or small. But they hit a small business harder, because there are
fewer bodies and assets to absorb the shock.

The key to our success lies in the ability to "open our hearts"
to discovery. Do we dread problems, or are we open to the
possibility that any challenge can actually become an opportunity?

The answer to that question may depend on how well we discover and use the power of our spirit.

Comfort barriers

Comfort barriers offer protection, but they also hold us back. The same wall that keeps us safe from the world also keeps us *from* the world.

We will have fewer surprises and dangers inside our comfort barriers. But opportunity is a camper; it likes to be outside. We can step outside of our comfort barriers and camp out with opportunity, if we know where to find our courage.

Growth

John says your spirit loves the danger of growth. Sometimes growth can be dangerous, but more often, *not* growing is the riskier alternative.

Small business owners "open their hearts to discovery" every day.

Each of us possesses the ability to be courageous or to be a weenie. Our spirit sees the possibility of success in the market-place, while the weenie in us sees the chance of failure. Our spirit says, "let's make something happen," while the weenie in us craves comfort.

Knowing how to manage these two forces is crucial to success in small business.

So how do you know when to grow? Listen to your spirit, then leverage that force.

Write this on a rock … Discover your spirit, trust it as a powerful force in you, step outside your barriers, and start camping out with opportunity.

Business life forms

In nature, all life can be reduced to two forms —plant and animal. In the marketplace, all business entities can be reduced to two forms—human and non-human.

The human entities are sole proprietorships and general partnerships. The non-human ones are legally formed, like corporations and limited liability companies (LLC).

The distinction is important for three primary reasons: legal issues, like contracts and lawsuits; perpetuity issues; and tax filing and tax paying.

In nature, a plant can't change its DNA and turn into an animal. But a sole proprietorship can morph into a non-human business entity, separate from its human shareholders.

Here are two benefits of forming a non-human entity:

1. A legal entity is formed which can enter into contracts, pay taxes, and be sold or inherited.
2. A "corporate veil" is established, which is a legal term for liability protection for the personal assets of corporate stockholders or LLC members.

When should you morph?

If your business isn't one of the non-human forms, should it be? If it's very small, you might be able to spend that $500-$1,000 expense on something more immediately critical, like a computer or marketing. But one concern is that you might wait until it's too late.

So how do you know when to morph? With organization and operating triggers, like any one of these examples:

- When you hire your first employee.
- When you enter into contracts.
- When you establish any credit.

Maintenance required

Non-human entities do require maintenance. Here are a few critical maintenance tips:

- Tell *everyone* that your business is formed as a non-human entity.
- Identify the legal ownership designation (like Inc.) on all documents and signage.
- Operate the entity with its own checking accounts.
- Maintain proper documentation, like shareholder and director meeting minutes.

If you fail to perform proper maintenance, you're at risk of having your corporate veil "pierced." This is another legal term for when someone with a claim against the company tries to go through the non-human entity to get to personal assets of shareholders.

Should your business be one of the non-human forms?

Think of the corporate veil as you do your roof: Maintaining both will protect you from dangerous things that fall from the sky, like hail and attorneys.

The big three

There are three primary non-human entities: C corporation, S corporation, and the Limited Liability Company. Talk with your attorney and CPA about which non-human form is right for you.

And finally don't forget the triggers: be intentional, not accidental about your business's life form, and keep up the maintenance on your non-human entity, which will vary by state.

Write this on a rock ... Your business is not a plant; you can change its DNA.

And God created the franchise

One of the questions often asked by some would-be entrepreneurs is, "What business should I go into?" These folks may have the passion to be a small business owner, but just not passionate about anything in particular.

Starting a business from scratch isn't for everyone. God understood this when he created the franchise.

Operating a franchise is entrepreneurial coloring inside the lines. You get the rush of working without a net, without having to come up with all the answers.

There are literally thousands of franchising options from which to choose: from auto repair to air filtering; carpet cleaning to car rental; hamburgers to home improvement. You get the picture.

The bad news is that the franchise universe is very large and intimidating. The good news is that the fundamentals you should apply to conduct your due diligence are basically the same, regardless of the industry you choose.

Franchising 101

My friend, Andrew Sherman, literally wrote the book on franchising. In *Franchising & Licensing*, he identifies several elemental components in any relationship between a franchisor— the developer of the franchise, and a franchisee—the purchaser of the franchise.

Understanding these elements will help you establish a strong foundation upon which you can build a successful franchise operation. Here are my thoughts on three of the important ones Andrew identifies:

1. A proven prototype.
This is franchising 101. Never pay money for a franchise

unless you *know* the model works. Period!

You must be able to replicate the product or service over and over again. And customers must be able to count on the same experience every time.

McDonalds may not have the best hamburger in the world, but whether you're in Moline or Moscow, you know it will taste just like the one you ate in Meridian.

2. A strong management and training team.

Check out the management team's credentials, including how long key members have been with the franchisor.

It's impossible to overstate how much support you're going to need. You'll have a thousand questions, and that's just the first day. So make sure your franchisor has its training stuff together.

Starting a business from scratch isn't for everyone.

3. Sufficient capitalization.

A franchisor is like any other business—it must have enough capital to support franchisees, innovate, grow, and weather storms. Your prospective franchisor will demand to know how financially solid you are, and you should require no less of them.

Franchises are like busses; if you miss this one, another will be along in six minutes. It's okay to get excited about a franchise. But whatever you do, don't fall in love until you finish the due diligence and have answers to all your questions.

Write this on a rock ... When the entrepreneurial sap rises in your bark, see if the world of franchising is for you.

Seeking efficiencies

Biutou Doumbia lives in a tiny village in the West African country of Mali. Biutou (sounds like Bee-oo-too) and her family live in poverty, very close to the line between survival and, well, you know.

Oh, one more thing: Biutou is a small business owner. She makes and sells peanut butter.

In Mali, peanut butter is made the same way African women have made other staples for millennia: by grinding the seeds on a rock with a large wooden pestle.

You might say that Biutou's operation is vertically integrated: She grows the peanuts and then manufactures, sells, and distributes her product.

Over two centuries ago, in *The Wealth Of Nations*, Adam Smith explained how markets are made by the division of labor. And free markets created capitalism, which Ayn Rand called, "the only system geared to the life of a rational being."

Biutou doesn't know Smith or Rand from a warthog—she's illiterate. But she is one of Rand's rational beings. And as such, she recognized the efficiencies of division of labor when a diesel-powered grinder/blender was made available.

Now, for 25¢ and a 10-minute wait, Biutou's 15 pounds of peanuts turn into better peanut butter than she could make pounding all day with a pestle.

Chocolate and vanilla

Biutou now practices intermediation—a fancy modern-day word for division of labor—which is the process of employing contractors to create efficiencies. It's a valid business strategy, as is its opposite—you guessed it—disintermediation: the process of removing vendor layers, usually to get closer to customers.

These two strategies are as different as chocolate and vanilla, but like ice cream, choosing one doesn't mean the other is wrong —just different.

Biutou had practiced disintermediation because she didn't have a choice. You have many choices, but are you choosing wisely?

Core competencies

One of the things every business must do today is focus on core competencies: *what you do that makes your business valuable to customers.* Everything else, theoretically, can be performed by a specialist in your non-core activity.

Take a look at your own operation to see if—like Biutou—you can find efficiencies and recover time through intermediation. Ask yourself and your staff this six-word question: *Must this task be done in-house?*

Your answer will be found in the answers to other questions like these:

You have many choices, but are you choosing wisely?

- How much control do we lose, and can we live with it?
- How much of not using intermediation is about ego?
- What impact will our decision have on customers?

Remember, any decision to employ intermediation—or not —should be driven by the desire to seek efficiencies and improve customer service.

Write this on a rock ... Take a lesson from Biutou: Use intermediation, but only when it's good for you and your customers.

What's the next step?

In the small business you have, or the one you want to start, what's the next step?

If you want to own your own business, where do you want to start? From home? A brand new start-up downtown? Or perhaps you want to buy an existing business.

If you already own your business, what's next? More product lines? More inventory? Bigger showroom? More branch offices? Take your company public?

I believe there are at least three things that motivate us to take that next step in business:

1. Our natural inclination as humans to want to improve our lives is well documented in history and abundantly evident in our contemporary world.

2. Our pride, competitiveness and ambition combine to compel us to reach for the next accomplishment.

3. Market forces, often associated with fear and greed, motivate us to take the next step.

As a business owner, the question is not *if* you will take the next step, because some combination of the three things listed above will motivate you to do that. The questions are *when* will that step happen, and *how big* will it be?

Here are two great quotes that have helped me make "next step" decisions.

Discretion is valuable

One of my favorite quotes from Shakespeare is from *Henry IV*. In Act V, Scene IV, Falstaff comically rationalizes his cowardice with this: "The better part of valor is discretion."

I think small business owners should memorize this handy line—not to rationalize cowardice, but rather to recognize the wisdom and value that can be found in discretion.

Whenever it looked like I was about to embark on a windmill-tilting expedition during a tenure with one of my mentors, he would slow me down by paraphrasing Falstaff with this question: "Do you have a fighting chance, or just a chance to fight?" One of the keys to success, I've decided, is in the ability to discern which of these chances is before you.

Aim high

The second great line that I would like to offer is from an unlikely source. We know Michelangelo Buonarroti as an

"The better part of valor is discretion."

invaluable contributor to the Renaissance period through his art and architecture, but not so much his philosophy.

Here's what this great master had to say about the question I asked you earlier: "The greatest danger for most of us is not that we aim too high and miss it, but that we aim too low and reach it."

Next time you have a business decision before you, write the Falstaff line at the bottom of a piece of paper, and then put Michelangelo's words at the top. Keeping both in view and in mind, write your decision in the middle. And don't forget to ask yourself if your decision will give you a fighting chance, or merely a chance to fight.

Write this on a rock ... Small business decisions must be made with generous portions of high aim *and* discretion.

Observing rare species

As you venture into the marketplace jungle, don't miss the opportunity to observe that rare, wild creature—the entrepreneur—in his or her natural environment.

You will find entrepreneurs to be different from others of their species. They have extraordinarily high levels of certain human traits that make them interesting to observe.

Here are some of the traits to look for in order to identify this elusive species:

Vision

Entrepreneurs can see things and imagine the possibilities before they even exist, often as the world is telling them, "It won't work." When entrepreneurs are deep into their vision mode, they go into what their families call "the zone." Observation note: It's easiest to slip up on them when they are in this zone.

Curiosity

Entrepreneurs ask questions no other human would. They can't help it, because at the core of any entrepreneur is a primordial desire to know how something works, sometimes even before that something is a thing.

If someone asks you a question and you have no idea what he's talking about, you may be having a close encounter of the third kind with an entrepreneur. Don't be irreverent. You might be at ground zero of the 21st century equivalent of Velcro, the microchip, or the margarita blender.

Courage

Entrepreneurs attempt things that others in their species won't. Bravery is doing something risky in the moment. Courage is taking the risk after you've had time to think about it.

As you peer through the marketplace triple canopy, look for

behavior in defiance of conventional wisdom. Entrepreneurs eat conventional wisdom for breakfast.

Tenacity

Three things about this characteristic: 1) Entrepreneurs have a high pain threshold; 2) they keep trying when other humans give up; 3) they have a visceral desire to nurture and protect their business that's rivaled in nature only by the maternal instinct. Combined, these three manifest in a primal tenacity that's often frightening to other humans.

If the entrepreneur you're observing is crouching tenaciously, lie down quickly. You probably aren't in danger, but fainting is a possibility.

Faith

Entrepreneurs believe in themselves and their vision. The great writer/curmudgeon, H.L. Mencken, once said, "Faith may

Entrepreneurs see things and imagine the possibilities.

be defined as an illogical belief in the occurrence of the illogical."

If you see someone demonstrating an inordinate commitment to an "illogical belief," congratulations—you've had an entrepreneur sighting.

When small business owners wake up in the marketplace, they're like an animal in the middle of the food chain waking up in the jungle—they don't know if they're going to eat today, or be eaten.

Even so, if you want to get close to entrepreneurs, darting them is not necessary; they're normally very gentle creatures. Just rub their stomachs—they like that.

Catch and release, please.

Write this on a rock ... Looking for a threatened species to love and protect? Consider the entrepreneur.

Your thoughts

_____

_____

_____

_____

_____

_____

_____

_____

_____

_____

_____

_____

_____

_____

_____

_____

_____

Planning for success

Here is a conversation that's conducted between business owners and their friends and acquaintances every day. After you "listen" to this visit, we'll talk about how to turn this conversation into an important management tool. By the way, our owner's name is Joe.

Friend: "Hi Joe. Heard you're starting a new business. What kind?"

Joe: "Oh, hi Jim. Yeah, John and I are going to be selling square widgets to round widget distributors."

Friend: "How're you going to do that?"

Joe: "We found out that no one has thought to offer square widgets to these guys. We asked around, and it looks like they not only need square widgets, but they will pay a premium for them."

Friend: "Sounds good. Where are you going to get your square widgets?"

Joe: "Well, we discovered that the round widget guys don't need first quality square widgets, so we're buying seconds, cleaning them up, repackaging them, and delivering them to those customers."

Friend: "Sounds like you've found a niche. How many can you sell in a year?"

Joe: "We've identified the need for 15,000 this year, and with the trend in the market, we think we can double that within three years. Gotta go. See ya later."

Saying your plan

Now, let's look at what just happened. In this two-minute conversation, the owner identified his business, management team, industry, business focus, market niche, customer profile, vendor profile, pricing strategy, market research results, and finally, his growth plans.

Probably without realizing it, Joe actually *said* his business plan. All that's left is to add a few other elements, plus the narrative and numbers.

And since you're having these conversations, too, that means you're saying *your* business plan—also probably without realizing it.

So, we know you're saying your plan, but are you getting it on paper so you can use it?

And if you're asking why you need a business plan, here are the three best answers: 1) To get a business loan; 2) to attract investors; and 3) because it's an essential management tool.

Don't wait until you need a business plan to start one.

Don't make these mistakes

- Don't wait until you need a business plan to start one.
- Don't wait until you have time.
- Don't make it harder than it has to be.

You can't eat fruit from a tree that was never planted, and you can't manage with a business plan that was never started. The first words of your plan are the seeds from which you will grow your business. So just start writing what you already know, like Joe's conversation.

One final point: There are computer programs that will help you produce your plan for under $100. But first, check out the free examples of business plans at this Web site: www.bplans.com.

Write this on a rock ... A written business plan will help you achieve new levels of management professionalism.

Our growth isn't genetic

Hundreds of years ago, the seed of a giant sequoia redwood tree took root. At that moment, it was genetically pre-determined that this tree would become, well, a giant.

If the germinating seed of a Bradford Pear tree could know anything, it's that its issue will never be very tall. As trees go, Bradford Pears are short. It's in the genes.

A tree's growth plan is fairly simple: Soak up sunshine, nutrients and water, fight off pests and competition, and let genetics take care of the rest.

This sounds kind of like our small businesses, doesn't it? Except for one thing: There is no genetic code to pre-determine a business's size. Whether a giant or an ornamental, it's up to us.

The growth questions

A Bradford Pear tree can't grow as tall as a redwood, but in a free-market economy, a business can be what the owner makes it. And for small business owners, that fact begs two questions that we go to sleep asking ourselves, and wake up trying to answer: Is it time to grow? And if so, how big?

But just as you have the ability to grow, you can also limit growth. And believe it or not, the latter is usually more difficult than the former. Here's why:

- Entrepreneurs are hard-wired to create more of the object of their entrepreneurial dreams.
- The culture of the marketplace encourages, recognizes, and rewards growth.
- The most prominent by-product of success is growth.

In the face of all of these pressures to grow, small business owners must be able to answer those two growth questions—

when and how big—plus one more: Why?

Growing is optional

Make sure you know *why* your business should grow, because growth for its own sake is organizational suicide.

Here are three dangerous lies that owners tell themselves to justify growing:

1. We can grow out of our organizational problems.
2. Growth = more profit.
3. When we grow, customers will benefit.

Here's the truth: Growth is a rope that will be made into either a ladder or a noose.

To help you answer the "Why?" question, here are five reality checks, each followed by a slap-in-the-face question.

There is no genetic code to pre-determine a business's size.

1. The marketplace is pretty full already. Is there a real opportunity to grow?
2. Growth takes cash. How will you fund yours?
3. The rewards of growth are typically delayed. Can your organization wait for the payoff?
4. Growth will take your operation into unfamiliar territory. Do you have the staff and systems to blaze that trail *and* take care of your customers?
5. Owning a business should be a source of happiness. Are you sure you'll be happy with a larger business?

This is the part where you say, "Thanks. I needed that." You're welcome.

Write this on a rock ... How big your business becomes is not genetically pre-determined. Just because you *can* grow doesn't mean you should. Good luck.

Laws of aggregation

Sakrete is one of the handiest products ever developed for those small do-it-yourself construction projects.

It's basically a bag of rocks and dust. But to a weekend warrior with a honey-do list, it can be a sack of magic.

Packaged in relatively small bags, Sakrete is an aggregation of cement mix, sand and different size gravel. When you stir in water and apply it, in time it becomes concrete.

So, what can small business owners learn from a sack of rocks? Plenty, actually.

There's the chemical reaction that the components have to one another when mixed with water. In order to become effective quickly and have lasting strength, both Sakrete and organizations must have the right chemistry.

But the most valuable lesson is in the aggregation. Sakrete doesn't just aggregate the correct material, but also different size material—from powder to sand to stones. The larger pieces provide substance and strength, while the smaller ones bind everything together and nimbly fill in where needed to eliminate weak spots.

In the marketplace, chemistry between people and organizations is pretty intuitive—if it's not right, we move on.

Aggregation is not so intuitive, which is why there are no Blasingame's Laws of Chemistry. But there are three Blasingame's Laws of Aggregation.

Blasingame's First Law of Aggregation: *Find your success in the aggregation of the success of your employees.*

Effective leaders hire smart people, train them well, provide them with the tools and information they need, give them both responsibility and authority, and show them how their success serves the organization's goals. But leaders who have enduring success, year after year, are those who feed their ego through the success of their employees. They celebrate that first, and their own accomplishments last.

Blasingame's Second Law of Aggregation:
Aggregation prevents aggravation.

In business, aggregation is also known as strategic alliances, which small businesses must build with other organizations, especially larger ones.

It's aggravating at least, and dangerous at worst, to manage threats and take advantage of opportunities without strategic resources. Consider the merits of forming a strategic alliance with an organization that already has what you need before you risk

What can small business owners learn from a sack of rocks?

the expense and possible delay of capitalizing the ownership of that resource.

Blasingame's Third Law of Aggregation: *Associate your brands with those that are better established.*

As you develop strategic alliances, look for partners with brands that have a higher recognition factor than yours, and arrange for the relationship to include your brand being presented in the marketplace alongside theirs. Brand association is smart aggregation.

Write this on a rock ... If you're not having the level of success you want, perhaps you should take an aggregation lesson from Sakrete.

An irony of the marketplace

Here's a scenario that plays out in the marketplace every day in Small Business, USA:

"My business is really growing these days," a small
business owner confides to his friend, "but we're still
experiencing too much negative cash during the month."

And then, with that deer-in-the-headlights look on his face,
he completes his concern: "I thought by now, with both sales and
profits up, that cash flow would be the least of my worries. I used
to be afraid I couldn't grow my business; now I'm worried that it
will collapse."

This entrepreneur's lament is one of the great ironies of the
marketplace: A small business in danger of failure as a result of
extreme success.

Blasingame's Razor

Beware Blasingame's Razor: *It's redundant to say, "undercapitalized small business."*

This maxim is especially true for growing small companies,
because sales volume growth depletes cash in two dramatic but
predictable ways:

1. When the business is growing, organizational upgrades
are to be expected in order to handle the new demands—new
vehicles, staff, technology, etc.—the possibilities are endless. Of
course, you must fund these things, often while the newfound
success is merely on paper and not yet in the bank.

2. Selling to customers on open accounts—where payment
for work or products is collected sometime after delivery —is
essentially making loans to customers. And while it's true that
your vendors may let you to do the same, typically they allow you
less time to pay than you allow your customers. This difference

between when you pay and when you collect creates a negative cash condition.

Here's how to manage these two challenges:

1. Growth plans must be compatible with the ability to fund that growth.

Too often we think that the big growth hurdle is to get customers to say yes. But you must consider the impact of sales growth on cash flow before delivering a proposal.

And don't be surprised if the answer to this equation shows that you actually have to turn down some business.

2. Don't use operating cash to fund acquisition of capital assets that have a life expectancy of more than two years.

**Blasingame's Razor:
It's redundant to say,
"undercapitalized
small business."**

Capital purchases should probably be funded by bank debt, and the interest you pay is the cost of Blasingame's Razor.

If you don't like debt, or paying interest, that should motivate you to leave profits in the business as retained earnings, which is the best way, ultimately, to overcome Blasingame's Razor.

3. Do a better job of collecting receivables on time.

Understanding the relationship between Accounts Receivable Days and Accounts Payable Days is an "Ah-ha!" moment for many small business owners. Successful growth cannot happen without monitoring this ratio very closely.

Write this on a rock ... If your business is growing nicely, congratulations. But beware Blasingame's Razor. It is possible for a small business to grow itself right out of business.

What was I thinking?

I know what I was feeling, but what was I thinking?!

This is the title lyric of a country song by Dierks Bentley. It's about a boy who lets a pretty face get him into a whole lot of trouble on their first date.

In matters of courtship, who hasn't done things—which we may have regretted the next day—that were impulsive and just plain boneheaded?

Of course, there's no accounting for this behavior when it comes to affairs of the heart. But when a small business owner says, "I know what I was feeling, but what was I thinking?" it probably results in the proverbial winged sack of money flying away.

Being passionate about starting a business is very important, but the business failure rate would drop like a stone if more prospective entrepreneurs understood that success in business requires more than desire: It takes knowledge of the industry, knowledge of business fundamentals—especially cash flow, and total commitment, in case the passion fades.

"I know what I was feeling, but what was I thinking?" is the post-passion lament of the passionate but too impulsive start-up business owner.

If you're not a start-up

For a more mature small business, "I know what I was feeling, but what was I thinking?!" may be less dangerous only to the degree that being established assumes some level of market penetration and critical mass.

This is not complicated: Fixing business mistakes costs money and, unlike a start-up, if you have customers, you're more likely, but by no means guaranteed, to be able to operate through the impact of a bad decision. A mentor once told me, "Sales will cure most business ills."

But why would seasoned business owners commit this rookie mistake? Often their post-passion lament is caused by ego or desperation.

When veteran business owners say "I know what I was feeling, but what was I thinking?" first look for a severe case of ego. The usual scenario is when someone who is good at one business deduces from that success that he or she can do anything.

Ego and capital

The road to business failure is paved with the assets of seasoned owners who didn't understand that in any new venture they should think of themselves as a start-up again, only this time with more to lose and possibly a runaway ego.

Mixing ego and capital, especially borrowed capital, is a dangerous cocktail that has taken down many a business.

Another mentor once told me, "Desperate people do desperate things."

Denial is the handmaiden of desperation.

Sometimes owners don't see market and industry shifts before it's too late. Sadly, in their desire to save their businesses, instead of believing their own eyes, they desperately seek "I know what I was feeling" solutions that conform to what they want to see.

But reality didn't get its name by being wrong, and "What was I thinking?" is the lament of the desperate. Denial is a powerful and seductive drug, and it's the handmaiden of desperation.

Write this on a rock ... In love, impulsiveness can be cute; in business, it's the straightest line to failure.

Balancing work and life

Work is essential as the activity that delivers the things necessary for our survival as humans.

Beyond survival, work is the lever of our intellectual curiosity and the blessing that has produced civilization.

If you're an employee, one day you expect to stop working and retire. In fact, many businesses have a mandatory retirement age in their employment policies.

But if you're a small business owner, it's likely that the concept of retirement takes on a much different perspective because, theoretically, you can work as long as you want.

Many of us love our businesses so much that we actually don't think about what we do as work. We're often so defined by our businesses that it may scarcely occur to us that we would ever stop working.

B.C. Forbes (1880-1954), founder of *Forbes* magazine and grandfather of Steve Forbes, said, "I have known not a few men who, after reaching the summit of business success, found themselves miserable upon attaining retirement age."

Mr. Forbes is warning us about the dangers of a life without balance, and his words have inspired this:

Blasingame's Small Business Balance Principle
The work you love can morph from blessing to curse if it exists without balance.

If you love your work, congratulations.

But simultaneous with that love, make sure you also love golf, or tennis, or—and this is a big one—your child's ball game, or whatever can become your work's counter-weight to balance the scales of your life.

Balance can make you beautiful

Research has shown that balancing our beloved work with other interests enhances physical and mental well-being, and actually increases productivity. And to others, it makes us much more interesting and desirable to know.

Balancing work and life is easier for employees than it is for an owner, because they typically have to be concerned only with their assignments.

But when the proverbial "buck" stops on the owner's desk, it's loaded up with all of the challenges and opportunities facing every aspect of the business. And even if you've acquired the ability to take all of this in stride, "all of this" quite simply just takes a lot of time. Consequently, balance requires more than awareness and conscious intention.

Finding the right combination of work and balance in the life of a small business owner requires the execution of at least three of the things that we use to achieve success in our businesses: planning, scheduling, and discipline.

The work we love can morph from blessing to curse if it exists without balance.

The virtues of having a balanced financial plan for retirement are self-evident. But we should be just as disciplined about balancing our work with other interests.

Otherwise, as Mr. Forbes observed, we may find ourselves "miserable upon attaining retirement age."

Write this on a rock ... The recipe for happiness includes love and experiences that create memories. Let's make sure our love and memories have balance.

Managing with trust

Are you familiar with the term "dysfunctional family?" The simple definition is a family whose members don't work and play well with each other. Such relationships typically create emotional, mental, sometimes even physical distress and/or estrangement.

Have you ever heard of a dysfunctional company?

If not, perhaps this definition will sound familiar: A dysfunctional company is one whose members don't work and play well with each other. Such relationships typically create emotional, mental, sometimes even physical distress and/or estrangement.

Someone once said, "Friends we choose—family we're stuck with." But what about business relationships; we certainly get to choose those, don't we?

The common denominator

So why are there dysfunctional businesses?

The answer is actually quite simple, and it's the common denominator in both businesses and families: human beings. If your family, or company, is dysfunctional, it's because of the behavior of the humans.

Humans aren't inherently bad, but we are inherently self-absorbed. And one of the by-products of self-absorption is self-preservation.

When self-preservation shields are up, mistrust flourishes, goals go unmet, and failure is likely. When shields are down, productivity, creativity, and organizational well-being are evident. But the latter only happens if it's believed that there is a basis for trust.

If your organization is not accomplishing its goals and making progress, look around to see if there is more self-preservation than teamwork going on . Where evidence of individual and   departmental self-preservation is found, you will also find lots of dysfunction, but not much trust.

A powerful force

In his book, *Built On Trust*, my friend, Arky Ciancutti, goes so far as to say that trust is "one of the most powerful forces on earth." He further states that the two most powerful trust-building tools are closure and commitment.

Closure is implied when a transaction ends with a promise to deliver by a stated time. Closure happens when performance, or a progress report, is actually delivered on time.

Look around to see if there is more self-preservation going on than teamwork.

Commitment, Arky says, "is a condition of no conditions." When the relationship between two parties is built on trust, there are no hidden agendas. And while commitment might not guarantee results, it does guarantee at least a progress report.

Even though closure and commitment are skills that often must be learned, you'll find willing participants in your employees, because human beings desire trust.

If your organization doesn't have a culture of trust, it's not the employees' fault. Leadership, trust and dysfunction all have one key thing in common: They're gravity fed. They all roll downhill.

Successful managers must learn trust-building skills, manage with them, and instill them in others. Create and maintain what your people desire—an organization built on trust.

Write this on a rock ... If organizational dysfunction is a poison, trust is its antidote.

Managing humans

Here's a question that will be on the test: How much of a typical small business's annual operating budget is set aside for training?

Answer: Not much—and more's the pity.

One of the most dramatic examples of a human resource lesson we should take from big business is in training. Far too many small firms conduct training after a fashion, if at all.

Historically, big businesses have had an advantage in this area because they have the resources to pay for structured training programs, and to give their people time away from their assignments to acquire training. But in the 21st century, things have changed.

Thanks to the Internet and thousands of companies that develop and distribute convenient and affordable online training programs, small businesses can acquire training in a wide range of fields without breaking the budget, and with a minimum of lost production.

Training is an excellent example of how technology has leveled the HR playing field for small businesses.

All employees are key

Now let's talk about success with our employees.

Wise owners understand that the best way to be outrageously successful is to first help employees be successful in their individual assignments and then recognize their progress. If this requires subordinating your ego and personal recognition to that of your employees, do it. Because remember *Blasingame's First Law of Aggregation*: All of that employee success ultimately aggregates for, and accrues to you, the owner.

Here's another question that will be on the test. Who are the key employees in a small business?

Answer: All of them.

Every employee in a small business must be competent, versatile and have a good attitude. Your company's ability to compete will be diminished by the same factor as the percentage of your employees who don't fit this profile.

Identify the keepers, praise them, equip them, train them, and pay them well. Get rid of everybody else.

Any questions?

Top small business challenges

What about employee acquisition and retention? Surveys show that these issues are only surpassed as a challenge for 21st century small businesses by providing health insurance for employees.

Whether the unemployment rate is zero or 10%, good people are *always* in demand. The best way to make sure you can find, hire and keep valuable employees is by making sure your company is a *great* place to work.

How do you do that? Practice the best human resources (HR) fundamentals, like those identified here, and you'll have the best people standing in line at your door with resumes in hand.

Far too many small firms conduct training after a fashion, if at all.

And that line will at least partially be created by word-of-mouth from your very happy and loyal employees.

Finally, now that you've hired smart, professional and competent people, make sure you listen to them.

Write this on a rock ... In terms of 21st century HR, thinking like the steward of your employees' success—instead of like a boss—is the straightest line to outrageous success for small business.

Motivating employees

Smart business owners know that there is a direct link between motivating employees to be successful in their assignments and the success of that business. Want a good example of why you should be one of these smart managers?

Let's imagine that your best employee has just resigned. How much will it cost—directly and indirectly—to find, hire, train, and get the replacement to that employee's productivity level? Scary, huh?

Now ask yourself if you could possibly be in jeopardy of losing good employees merely because you aren't properly motivating them in their assignments.

There are many ways to successfully motivate employees. All of them require managers to focus on the human beings with whom they work, and who desire to be successful themselves. Here are six of the most important ones.

1. Communication

There's nothing more fundamental to having productive, loyal employees than good communication. If you're having problems keeping employees, the low-hanging-fruit for you may be to just start talking *with*—not to—your people.

2. Professionalism

This is the aggregation of business, ethical and interpersonal behavior, and it's critical to successful employee motivation. It's a motivating force that fosters pride and employee loyalty.

Demonstrate your professionalism first, then help your employees become professionals themselves. And be sure to recognize them as they make progress.

3. Management style

Do you motivate employees by leading or driving them?

Drivers are managers who disregard others and consume people as a means to their end. They can be identified by high employee turnover.

Leaders value their people and encourage them to be successful. They can be identified by the double-digit numbers representing how many years their employees have been with them, and the multiple digits in black—to the left of the decimal on their bottom lines.

4. Employee training

Training pays motivational dividends. It fosters knowledge, which fosters self-confidence, which fosters leadership, which fosters employee loyalty, which fosters customer loyalty. Could there possibly be a straighter line to return on investment?

Help your employees to become professionals themselves.

5. Share recognition

A robin noticed a turtle sitting on top of a fence post. When the robin stopped to ask how he got there, the turtle replied, "Obviously, not by myself."

When talking about what your company has done, be sure to manage your pronouns properly. Whenever "I" can be replaced with "we," do it.

This tiny two-letter pronoun is a powerful little verbal high-five that will resonate motivational energy throughout your organization.

6. Have fun

Make sure your organization finds ways to have fun at work.

Write this on a rock … Motivating employees to be successful in their assignments is not only good business, it's also the right thing to do.

Democratic ironies

One of the great ironies is that while businesses flourish best in a democracy, a business cannot flourish as a democracy.

By definition, in a democracy stakeholders vote on issues and the majority rules. But while this process is one of the greatest developments of mankind with many applications, business is not one of them.

Pure democracy isn't practical in government, either.

But a group of visionary malcontents solved that problem over 200 years ago by creating something new: a democratic republic. Since then, Americans have elected a few to represent the interests of all, with understandable deference to the majority.

A business can be like a republic in that someone has to be the final decision-maker: one desk, as President Truman so famously said, where the proverbial buck stops.

No tyrants zone

Here's another irony: A business functions best when structured like a dictatorship, but not if managed by a tyrant.

And while the default structure of a business may look like a dictatorship, that doesn't have to dictate (no pun intended) how people are managed.

The dominator management model—as old as humanity itself—requires subordinates to dutifully follow the instructions of superiors. But this model is a withering vestige of centuries past and not currently competitive.

The 21st century management model must look more like a partnership. Just as effective government requires that democratic principles be augmented with outsourced representation, the necessity for an ultimate decision-maker in a business must be alloyed with the experience and brainpower of employees.

The Founders envisioned a nation that could be as dynamic as it was enduring, and as powerful as it was benevolent, but only if the stakeholders believed their investment in such an ideal was, and remained, valuable. The democratic republic—warts and all —essentially did this.

And even though Americans outsource the management of their government, the classic principles of democracy come to bear with regularly scheduled elections to see if the majority wants to change its mind.

Employees vote with their feet

Employees change their minds by seeking work elsewhere. And while they always had the right to leave a job that's managed by tyrants rather than leaders, many Americans in past generations swallowed their pride in favor of regular income, benefits and what we now know was the illusion of job security.

The 21ˢᵗ century management model looks like a partnership.

Today, employees have no such illusions. And while they accept the reality that managers have to make final decisions, they also expect to contribute to the basis for those decisions.

In the 21ˢᵗ century, a business still can't be structured as a democracy. But today, employees expect to be led, not driven; they want to contribute, not just take orders.

Managers still must make the ultimate decisions, but only after sharing the decision-making process with employees.

Write this on a rock ... Having the power to make final decisions isn't a license to be a tyrant.

Impatience is standard equipment

One of the markers of American culture is the sticker glued on the window of a new car. This document helps the shopper by listing the standard equipment and options on each vehicle plus, of course, the manufacturer's suggested retail price, or MSRP.

But what if you're shopping for an entrepreneur?

This may sound silly, but prospective employees do it all the time. So, what would be on that sticker?

We're not interested in the MSRP because, as MasterCard might say, entrepreneurs are priceless. What we're looking for is the list of standard equipment.

Naturally, this list would include things like courage, creativity, perseverance, determination and motivation. But one feature that is typically not found on the list of standard equipment for most entrepreneurs is patience.

"I'm patient! Darn it!"

Entrepreneurs have many redeeming characteristics, but patience is rarely one of them. And our only redemption is that we're more intensely impatient with ourselves than anyone or anything else.

The reason for this self-directed impatience is because seeking excellence requires that we demand much of ourselves. Unfortunately, in our quest we can also be too impatient with those on whom we most depend—our key employees.

And while impatience with ourselves can be constructive, it has the potential to produce adverse results when directed at our people.

But when you think about it, impatience with key personnel is actually pretty understandable. They show up every day, just like us; they work hard, just like us; and they're dedicated, just like us. Certainly such evidence of commitment creates the impression that they are—just like us.

And for many key employees it's not just an impression. They are committed or they would work somewhere else.

They can't read your mind

The problem occurs when we're impatient with our people because they didn't read our minds.

The road to business failure is paved with the stories of key people who left because someone mistook commitment for ESP. And any employer lacking this understanding will have key employees wishing they had traded up when they first checked out the sticker on their entrepreneur.

So how do entrepreneurs avoid destructive impatience? Communication.

We must communicate our plan, strategy and vision to our employees. We cannot demand as much of our staff as we do of ourselves if they don't have access to the same information we do.

Entrepreneurs have many redeeming characteristics.

In 1776, General George Washington said, "We must make the best of mankind as they are, since we cannot have them as we wish."

Effective communication skills will eliminate the need to find employees who are mind readers. Plus it will make employees more productive, since they won't have to spend so much time trying to make the best of us.

Write this on a rock ... Patience may not be standard equipment on an entrepreneur, but effective communication practices should be.

Fundamental financials

Business owners must always be diligent financial managers. There are too many fundamentals to list here, but consider these critical ones:

- Track sales-to-expense ratios each month, so you know if, when, and how much to adjust spending.

- Scrutinize inventory total volume, unit quantities and line distribution.

- Know your Accounts Receivable and Accounts Payable aging reports like the back of your hand. Understand the A/R-A/P relationship and how it affects cash requirements.

- Remember that every dollar of retained earnings is making you money, because it's working capital you don't have to borrow from the bank, or take from investors.

Two species

Now let's talk about the two species of small business owners: those who produce regular (at least quarterly) balance sheets and profit-and-loss statements (P&L), and those who don't.

If you're a member of the second species, and the only financial reports you have are the P&L and balance sheet you get once a year with your tax return, using that information to manage your business is like making a salad with 15-month old lettuce. In either case, what you're working with is rotten.

With the accounting software available today, there is no excuse for not producing, and managing with, current financial reports. These programs cost as little as a dinner for two, and anyone who can operate a computer can learn how to use them. The direct benefit is the essential ability to manage your business with fresh financial records.

What're you going to do with them?

Like the dog that chased the car and caught it, when you get your financials, do you know what to do with them? In addition to tracking individual line items, you must also understand their relationships to each other. For example:

An increase on the sales line is usually a good thing, but do you know where to look for a possible negative impact? If your bottom line is red, do you know where to find the impediment to profitability?

Every dollar of retained earnings is making you money.

Clearly, business failures could be significantly reduced if prospective owners were required to pass a course on how to read and understand financial statements, and especially the relationship between cash flow and accounting.

The more you educate yourself on the financial fundamentals and practice using them as they apply to your business, the more you will achieve operating excellence and financial success for your company.

Here's some tough love: If you can't pass the course mentioned above, don't start a business until you can. And if you can't pass the course but already own a business, I hope the cold sweat popping out on your forehead right now will motivate you to start your financial education immediately.

Write this on a rock ... Even if you have employees to manage the financial duties, you cannot delegate the ultimate responsibility for your business's financial performance.

The clocks of small business

Ti-i-i-ime is on my side, yes it is.

So sang the legendary Rolling Stones lead singer, Mick Jagger. As lyrics in a ballad, this is a nice sentiment, even romantic. But in small business, it's hogwash.

In the marketplace, there are actually three clocks at work: one for operating expenses, one for sales and one for cash. Rarely are any on the side of a small business.

The clocks that tick on sales and cash collections often seem to have hands that drag or even get stuck, while the clock that is in control of expenses is so well oiled and finely tuned that the hands seem to fly around the face. Let's take a look at the three clocks of small business.

Operating expense clock

Every month, like clockwork—whether sales are good, cash collections are on schedule, or profits exist—payroll must be met, rent must be paid, taxes must be remitted, plus phone bills, utilities, insurance premiums, etc., *ad nauseum*, must also be paid.

The Operating Expense Clock is hardwired to Greenwich, England for accuracy within a nanosecond per millennium, and nothing stops it short of a global, thermonuclear holocaust, coinciding with a direct hit from Halley's comet.

The only way to influence this clock is through operating efficiencies—you won't be billed for something you don't buy.

Sales clock

This clock runs off of the customer relationships you've created so that sales result each month. You project when each sale will occur by qualifying prospects and attributing a "clock" to each potential transaction so that you can budget future sales volume.

The Sales Clock is completely logical and intuitive: A sale will be made only when a prospect's purchase requirements have been met.

Cash clock

What is not so logical or intuitive is the Cash Clock and its relationship with the other two Clocks. Think of it like this: Cash is to sales as snow is to winter: You can have winter without snow, but you can't have snow without winter; you can have sales without cash receipts, but you can't have cash receipts without sales. And, of course, expenses are like the weather—you get some every day.

But what every small business owner knows is that for every single glitch in the mainspring of the Sales Clock, there are 100 sprocket failures that can slow or stop the Cash Clock. Consequently, it requires constant attention and maintenance.

In the marketplace there are actually three clocks at work.

Murphy's Law flourishes inside the Cash Clock and is a frequent resident in the Sales Clock. But the Operating Expense Clock is totally immune to Mr. Murphy's insidious law, and rocks on just like The Rolling Stones.

Write this on a rock ... In small business, time is only on our side when all three of our Clocks are closely managed, finely tuned and running perfectly.

Dashboard management

Here's a trick question: If your business were a car, would the dashboard instruments have gauges with needles you can monitor, or warning lights that flash with no specific information?

If you said flashing lights, that means you probably won't know your business has a problem until some damage is done.

The correct answer is gauges. And in your business those gauges are financial statements and operating ratios.

Let's take a look at three issues on two different business dashboards— first with warning lights and then with gauges.

Inventory light: *Warning! Check Inventory!*

If you're operating with an inventory light, by the time it flashes, your inventory is not only too high, but also poorly distributed across your lines. You may have lots of stuff on the shelf and in the warehouse, but not enough of what customers are buying now.

Inventory gauge

With a balance sheet inventory gauge, when you see inventory creeping up in any month, you can immediately adjust stocking levels to get them back in line.

Inventory is cash you can't spend until a customer pays for it. With cash so tight, can you wait for a light to flash before you make inventory decisions?

Payroll light: *Caution! High payroll!*

If your instrument panel has a payroll light, it will only flash when payroll expenses are already too high. By then, you may have made payroll commitments you can't justify and/or paid yourself a large bonus.

Payroll gauge

The needle on the payroll gauge identifies the payroll-to-sales ratio, including a breakdown of how much you should pay sales, management, production, etc.

Payroll is usually your largest operating expense. Do you want to manage it with the incremental movement of a needle, or wait for a light to come on?

Growth light: *Danger! Excessive speed!*

This light only comes on when your company's working capital pistons have reached red-line operating levels. By that time, either your internal systems will be over-extended, you will have grown yourself out of business, or both.

Growth gauge

Certain financial ratios are the growth gauges that indicate if you have the working capital required to expand, or if you should slow down until you've acquired the capital to grow successfully.

If your business were a car, would the dashboard have gauges or warning lights?

With your success depending on sound growth decisions, don't you need the incremental immediacy of a gauge?

Business gauges are the numbers on your financial statements and the ratios they produce. Like gauges on a car's instrument panel, when displayed accurately and checked regularly, they move in small increments to show positive trends, or warn you of specific impending dangers.

Astute business operators not only manage the movement of their operating gauges, but also understand the cause-and-effect relationship each gauge has with another.

Write this on a rock ... Business journeys are more successful when your company's dashboard has gauges instead of warning lights.

For profit, focus on the letters

Want to make this year a good profit year and next year even better? Think three letters: FOF. Focus on fundamentals

Operating Fundamentals are almost as old as the division of labor, which gave birth to the marketplace when shells were the currency of choice. Let's look at some of them.

Financial statements — Become an expert at understanding your financial statements. Spend more time with the numbers that are below the sales line on your operating statement. This is essential!

Budgets — Yuck, right? But operating fundamentals work best with a track to run on. Creating budgets won't be hard—sticking to them will be. Get on the track!

Cash management — When business slows down the first casualty is cash flow, not profits. You must be intimately familiar with your cash picture—don't delegate this!

Inventory — Inventory is a euphemism for cash. Find a way to convert into cash all inventory that is not turning. If you haven't been practicing Just-In-Time inventory management, do it now!

Customers — Categorize them from the most profitable As, to the least profitable Ds. Worship the As, cater to the Bs, encourage the Cs, and let the Ds learn the meaning of self-service. You might even have to fire a few. Really.

Products — Same song, different verse: A-B-C-D. Stock the fast-turning As and keep many of the Bs handy, but only a few of the Cs. What about the Ds? Never let one spend the night under your roof, unless it's been paid for!

Vendors and suppliers — If your sales volume is off, so is theirs. Ask them to help you manage inventory, maximize margins, lower freight costs, and develop new ways to support and serve your customers. If a vendor isn't part of the solution, get rid of them!

Systems — These are the structured components in your operation, some of which may now be outdated and unproductive. Scrutinize employee schedules, delivery routes, opening hours, etc. Nothing is sacred!

Add value — Find out what your customers need instead of trying to get them to take what you need to sell. If you don't add value to your customers' operations, you won't be successful in the 21st century marketplace!

Employees — Listen to your employees and let them help you find efficiencies and opportunities. Encourage creativity and entrepreneurial thinking. Invest in training. Share your plan and let them help you accomplish it. Cultivate producers and cut the dead wood!

Focus on fundamentals that are almost as old as the division of labor.

Bankers — Don't be a stranger. Bankers can help you if they're armed with your information—positive or negative. But remember: A banker without information is a scared banker, and no one ever got any help from a scared banker!

If you focus on these operating fundamentals, at year-end you may find that you were profitable, even if you had lower sales volume. And regardless of whether the economy is good or not-so-good, you'll be in a position to be profitable and have all the shells you need.

Write this on a rock ... Increase your profit potential by focusing on the fundamentals.

Focus on happiness

Why is happiness an operating fundamental? Because it's often difficult to tell where a small business stops and its owner starts. Truth is, there are times when being one with your business is not only a good thing, it's essential.

But extreme commitment weaves a fine seam between business and owner, which can produce a kind of single-mindedness that too often results in danger for the business and unhappy humans.

If you became a small business owner to find financial success, I'm not going to rain on your parade. As a capitalist, I admire that motivation.

But if you think being a rich business owner will make you happy, get your umbrella out, because wealth only provides options, not a guarantee of happiness. If you can't be happy without wealth, you won't be happy with it.

The best way to be a wealthy *and* happy small business owner is to be able to define success in more ways than just money and stuff.

A patchwork quilt

A small business is more like a patchwork quilt than a gilded security blanket. Some patches represent good things and some not so good; some patches are about the business, others are about the owner, and some are hard to tell. The happiest small business owners are those who find a way to feel successful regardless of which patch is before them.

Having multiple touchstones of success helps keep the rough patches in business and life in proper perspective. For example, measure success as much by the professional development of your employees as your net profit.

Place as high a value on being able to attend a child's school activity in the middle of the day as you do in getting a new contract. And be as proud of giving back to your community—or any worthy cause to which you contribute time and resources—as you are of the reason you can give back, your business's financial strength.

Just as man does not live by bread alone, entrepreneurs should not live by business alone.

Don't forget to have fun

Now let's talk about fun.

Reasonable people disagree on where we will spend eternity, but most agree that this is our only trip through this life. And every moment that goes by without some kind of joy is an opportunity lost.

You're no doubt planning for success this year, but have you made any plans to have fun?

If you can t be happy without wealth, you won t be happy with it.

Not your trip to Disney World. Are you having fun on any given day as you buy, sell, manage your business, and make   payroll?

The most successful business owners I know are the ones who have learned how to run a tight ship while being able to laugh and have fun.

Here's a flash: It is possible to run a successful business where the people laugh and find joy in their work.

And one more thing: Don't forget to laugh at yourself—in front of others. Those are usually the best laughs of the day.

Write this on a rock … Learn how to define success in more ways than just money and stuff. And don't forget to have fun.

Your thoughts

_____

_____

_____

_____

_____

_____

_____

_____

_____

_____

_____

_____

_____

_____

_____

_____

IP: Do you get it?

One of the most interesting aspects of the marketplace is the evolution of how businesses leverage assets.

For most of the history of the marketplace, business leverage came from the three basic categories below, listed in order of appearance as well as their historic market value:

1. Muscle power (whether human or animal)
2. Tangible stuff (raw material, inventory, tools, etc)
3. Information (today we call this intellectual property, or IP for short).

Historically, the strongest cavemen, the biggest horses, the fastest ships, and the largest factories all had an advantage over lesser competitors. And in the world of small business, it sounded like this: "We have the largest inventory in the area."

But here's the interesting part: as the marketplace has evolved, the order of importance and the value of assets has inverted. Studies show that marketplace participants place an increasingly higher value on IP and the ability to leverage it than on tangible assets.

And what about muscle power? In most of the global marketplace, it has become number four on a list of three.

Don't get left behind

The good news is that small businesses are joining this global trend by leveraging IP more and tangible assets less.

They're using technology in exciting new ways, doing more virtual business, and are as likely today to develop a strategy for doing business across an ocean as they were across town 20 years ago.

Regarding the power of IP and how essential it is to their

business's ability to be competitive in the 21st century, more and more, small businesses "get it." The bad news is there still are far too many who don't—and in the global marketplace, they're becoming less competitive.

Four trick questions

1. If I gave you, free of charge, either a truckload of inventory or a unique system of delivering your product or service that no one else had, would you take the inventory or the information?

2. Do you spend more time thinking about your products and services, or finding and employing technology and systems to more effectively and efficiently deliver your products and services?

> *As the marketplace has evolved, the order of importance and the value of assets has inverted.*

3. Do your employees use less technology in the direct performance of their jobs today compared to ten years ago, or more?

4. If you were purchasing a business, which would be more valuable to your future success: the inventory and the business equipment, or the electronic customer information the seller has amassed about who their customers are, how to contact them, what they buy, why they buy it, when they want it, and how they use it?

If you chose the first option to any of these questions, to paraphrase Jeff Foxworthy, you might be a caveman.

But if you chose the second options, congratulations—YOU GET IT!

Write this on a rock ... In the 21st century, advantage goes to businesses that leverage intellectual property more, and tangible assets less.

Your next killer app

An application, according to Webster, is "putting to practical use." In commercial terms, it's a capability developed to leverage a broader development, commodity, or system. Tea bags are an application developed to take advantage of the demand for that commodity.

The killer application—or killer app, for short—is the Holy Grail of entrepreneurs. According to the *Computer Desktop Encyclopedia*, a killer app is "an application that is exceptionally useful or exciting."

That was then

The incandescent light bulb, the Model T, the Xerox copier, Microsoft Windows, and the Web browser are examples of useful and exciting killer apps.

Depending on whether you are creating one or are in the crosshairs of one, a killer app can at once be exciting and threatening; create opportunity while wreaking havoc; give birth to a paradigm shift and—as the name seems to imply—be the death of an old order.

Killer apps have created new markets and destroyed old ones; launched opportunistic corporate ships and sunk hidebound corporate relics; built wealth while simultaneously destroying fortunes.

A new killer app?

In the 1990s era of irrational exuberance, everyone was looking for the next killer app. But are there any killer app opportunities for small business in the 21st century? Absolutely, especially if we can re-think the definition.

A killer app is an application that is exceptionally useful or exciting. Do you see anything in these words to indicate scale?

Where does it say that a killer app has to be any particular size? And there's nothing in there about a killer app having to change the world.

A small business killer app is the unique capability you create that increases your competitive advantage by maximizing your value to customers.

How do you create a killer app? Two relatively simple steps: Ask customers what they need, and then leverage technology to give it to them.

This is now

The new economy is real, but it's more about new tools than new rules. Those new tools (technology) are ready for small business owners to employ to create their own kind of killer apps. And you can even rent the new tools you need, when you need them, without having to "go public" to be able to afford them.

Are there any killer app opportunities left for small business?

In Henry Ford's day, sustained growth over a number of years meant you would one day stop being a small business. With the incremental availability of technology and online resources, the killer apps you create today allow you to grow year after year without becoming big in the traditional sense, unless you want to.

And unlike the "dot bombs" of the 1990s, new killer apps typically have that boring, old economy thing going for them—profitability.

Write this on a rock ... Think of it: Big business capability with the simplicity and nimbleness of a small business. You can achieve that quest with your very own small business killer apps. Now that's my idea of a Holy Grail!

Focus on technology

Early in the 1960s movie, "The Graduate," Dustin Hoffman's character, Benjamin Braddock, is celebrating his college graduation. Perhaps the most famous line in the movie is when an older friend offers this advice: "Ben, one word—plastics."

Consider this your small business graduation party: I have one word for you—technology.

Technology is one of the three most important 21st century levers you can use to grow your small business, along with networking and strategic alliances. If you disagree, answer these two questions:

Would you like to be able to compete—straight up—with a much larger company? Would you like your business to become integrated in the operation of large customers?

One word

If you answer yes to either question, I have one word for you —technology.

Below are some thoughts on using technology, followed by how *not* to use it.

Are you doing your accounting on a computer? Are you managing prospect development and customer relationships electronically? Do you have an automated inventory tracking system? Can customers check availability and order status without talking to one of your employees? Are you buying postage and overnight courier services online? If not, I have another word for you—Why?

Powerful technological operating resources are no longer out of reach of small business. They're available, affordable, and they work.

Growing the top line of your P&L is nice, but what you're

really after is making the number on the *bottom line* bigger. Watch net profit jump when you grow sales *and* improve operating efficiencies through the leveraging of technology, instead of hiring more people.

Small businesses create most of the new jobs, but that's not why we're in business. Whether planning for growth, seeking efficiencies, or both, think technology first and increasing payroll second.

Technology and customers

Now that you're committed to leveraging technology at all operational levels, let me temper that strategy by paraphrasing a critical theme of John Naisbitt's 1982 landmark book, *Megatrends*. With customer relationships, the wonders of high tech are no substitute for the value of high touch.

I have one word for you—technology.

Making customers use your technology just because it's good for you is a cardinal sin of the 21st century.

Use technology to find customers, serve customers, and manage customer relationships. But customers should only touch technology if it benefits them, in which case it comes across as productive, progressive, helpful, and even cool.

Remember what we've said about the rude reality of customer relationships: It's all about them. Or as they would say, "WIIFM: What's in it for me?"

Any technology that doesn't deliver an acceptable answer to that prime question should never touch a customer.

Write this on a rock ... One word—technology. Any questions?

Think price — not wages

Many small businesses sell professional services —like consulting, desktop publishing and Web site development —rather than a tangible product. And the big issue for these entrepreneurs is how to establish a price for their work.

Unfortunately, too often they do it poorly.

If you're a personal service provider, don't make the professionally fatal mistake of comparing what you charge your clients to how much you made as an employee. Doing so, to paraphrase Mark Twain again, is like comparing lightning to a lightning bug.

Many issues come into play when deciding what to charge for your intellectual product. But a good starting point is the method used to price tangible products: Begin with your cost of goods, which for you is what you want to be paid as an employee of your business. Then calculate the hourly rate to charge clients based on the gross profit needed to cover *all* operating expenses, *all* taxes, and finally, produce a net profit.

Three reasons

1. You're a business now. Businesses have price lists, not wage lists, and they collect revenue, not a paycheck.

2. As a professional services business owner, you're going to work *more* than 40 hours a week, but you may not always be able to actually *bill* 40 hours a week.

   You'll have to do all the administrative stuff, plus marketing, delivering proposals and providing initial interviews with prospects. Consequently, your business must collect enough revenue to cover the unbillable time you spend on those tasks, or the expense of paying someone else to do them for you.

3. Until you can bring other professionals into the business to increase company revenue, you're a 100% extension of yourself. Which means your only revenue leverage is what you charge per hour.

By now you should be getting the picture—mathematically, chronologically and organizationally—why consultants and other deliverers of professional services must charge more than wages.

Rent-a-professional

You should think like a rental car company that charges $50 a day to use one of its vehicles. That works out to $1,500 a month for a car that you could own for $350 a month, but you understand that you're paying a premium for the strategic availability.

Deliverers of professional services must charge more than wages.

You have a temporary transportation need, the rental company delivers the product and service just in time, and you give it back whenever your need has been fulfilled, without further obligation. No muss, no fuss—like when a client rents your professional services.

As a professional for rent, the services you provide and the resource that you are to your clients means they don't have to adopt you, like an employee. They can rent you and send you on your way after your "product" is delivered.

Write this on a rock ... Price your personal services like a business prices a tangible product, not like an employee thinks of wages.

Professional vitamin C

For centuries, prolonged service at sea often resulted in a malady called scurvy. Sailors so afflicted bruised easily and had joint pain, gum disease, tooth loss —you get the picture.

In the mid-18th century, researchers discovered that sailors given citrus fruit, like lemons and limes, did not get scurvy. We now know that the active ingredient in this "remedy" is vitamin C, also known as ascorbic acid. Ascorbic actually means "no scurvy."

One of the maladies often found in business owners is a condition I call "professional scurvy." This kind doesn't cause your teeth to fall out, but symptoms do include high levels of negative energy, low levels of performance, and an easily bruised ego, all of which manifest in a dangerous, and sometimes professionally fatal, failure-to-success ratio.

The good news is, like the seagoing kind, professional scurvy can be cured with vitamin C—actually four kinds of Professional Vitamin C.

1. Vitamin Courage

Challenges ignored will turn into ugly problems that can bruise a business. But facing a challenge with courage will reduce the negative impact and give it a chance to morph into an opportunity.

Courage is being brave *after* you've had time to think about it. Here's more good news: Most challenges allow enough time for you to think about them and apply a healthy dose of Vitamin Courage.

2. Vitamin Confidence

Didn't Thomas Edison say failure is successfully identifying what doesn't work? Pure success tends to build ego, which in high concentration can be professionally dangerous. But success alloyed with failure actually builds confidence, which is essential for long-term performance.

Vitamin Confidence in business is nothing more than faith in your ability to sail around present and future challenges—as well as seize the opportunities that come your way.

3. Vitamin Character

Contracts are the transactional laws of the marketplace. But in business, like the captain and crew of a sailing ship, it's the character of the parties that ultimately make a relationship work, not just the words or signatures on paper.

Those who demonstrate high levels of Vitamin Character— like doing the right thing even if the contract doesn't require it— don't have difficulty finding customers or crew.

Courage is being brave after you've had time to think about it.

4. Vitamin Credential

This one is critical, because courage without skill is the definition of foolhardy; confidence without resources is what Texans call, all hat and no cattle; and character without knowledge is a well-intentioned commitment that probably can't be kept.

All the best intentions won't make your business successful if you don't acquire adequate levels of Vitamin Credential— education, skill, experience, and resources—that can back up your business plan and commitment to deliver.

Write this on a rock ... Preventing professional scurvy is no longer a mystery. All it takes is liberal doses of the four kinds of Professional Vitamin C.

Customer? What Customer? Part I

The following advice from an unknown author once came across my desk.

"It is essential to know at all times what your competition is doing, or you might lose old accounts and new prospects."

Fundamentally, this advice is sound. But it becomes dangerous when a company is *obsessed* with the competition.

Alas, there is evidence that obsession with the competition is becoming an unfortunate operating trend. I call this trend the "Customer? What Customer? Syndrome," or CWCS, for short.

A company has CWCS when it is more likely to ask, "What is my competition doing?" rather than the much more important question, "What do my customers want?"

There are two levels of CWCS. Level One afflicts employees when the company focus is not on the customer. You see CWCS all the time.

A fast food employee shoves a sack of burgers at you without looking up or saying anything; no smile, no "Thanks for your business." That's CWCS.

Here's another one: When three employees at a mall store can't break away from their very important chat to make sure you find what you're looking for, you've just been a drive-by victim of CWCS.

One more: You call or go by a business to get help with something that they should have taken care of. Afterwards, you thank the employee who helped you, who then says, incredibly, "No problem." You were just slimed by CWCS.

Let's rewind

Let's rewind these three scenarios and correct the responses. In the first example, the proper behavior is direct eye contact, a sincere smile, and a simple but powerful "Thank you."

In the second situation, since virtually every retail purchase is preceded by "Just looking," no chatting is allowed when customers are present.

And finally, in the third scene, instead of "No problem"—which has to be one of the worst things to ever say to a customer—how about "I'm very sorry you had this problem. Thank you for allowing us to make it right. What else can we do for you?"

Organizations with Level One CWCS commit plenty of resources to stay one step ahead of the competition in products, pricing and marketing. But if training happens at all, it's usually to sell "at" customers, rather than take care of them. Sadly, often there is no training, which allows CWCS to occur naturally, but with the same unfortunate results.

It's dangerous when a company is obsessed with the competition.

CWCS is preventable

The good news is Level One CWCS is absolutely preventable. All it takes is hiring the right people and training them to focus on customers, not on the competition.

One more thing: Management has to operate the business so that employees believe the company is focused on delivering to customers what they really want, rather than manipulating customers in order to beat the competition.

This leads us to Level Two CWCS, which we will discuss in the next chapter. Level Two only afflicts executives.

Write this on a rock ... Knowing the competition is a key sales fundamental, but focusing on the customer is the prime operating fundamental.

Customer? What Customer? Part II

In the last chapter, you were introduced to CWCS, which stand for "Customer? What Customer? Syndrome." This condition is found in companies that are more concerned with competitors than with customers.

You learned that Level One CWCS infects employees who have received little or no training about the direct link between customers and their employer's success—or even their paychecks. Level One is dangerous but not hopeless, because those so afflicted can be cured with training.

Now let's talk about Level Two CWCS, which only afflicts executives.

Level Two is more troubling and organizationally more devastating because it occurs at the top, where strategic decisions are made.

The incidence of Level Two CWCS is not associated with company size or structure; it afflicts owners of small businesses as well as managers of multi-national conglomerates.

Like Level One, the cause of Level Two is simple, but it is different: Level Two is caused by a change in proximity.

Competitors vs customers

As a business grows, it's a natural law that executives become more involved in the macro operating issues, which almost by definition puts them in closer proximity to competitors than to customers. When competitors become more top-of-mind and customers are more out-of-sight and out-of-mind, Level Two CWCS occurs, and it looks like this:

Decisions are made that favor strategies focused more on manipulating customers away from competitors than on creating a unique customer experience, including training employees how to deliver that experience.

Executives with CWCS see their job as a game where increasing marketshare means they've beaten a competitor, instead of executing best practices that create customer loyalty by adding value to their customers' experiences.

A company infected with CWCS uses its size or market presence to try to intimidate customers to do business with them, instead of developing strategies that create the long-term benefit of having customers they can't run off.

It's actually possible for an entire industry to contract CWCS. It happens when companies have obsessed about each other so much that, in time, it becomes difficult to tell them apart. Such a scenario is fertile soil for entrepreneurs. Witness the competitive landscape of the airline industry, for example.

Level Two CWCS is not associated with size or structure.

A CWCS vaccine

How do you inoculate for CWCS? With the "There's My Customer!" vaccine, or TMC.

The TMC formula is simple, inoculation is fun, and the ROI is enormous: Spend more time asking what your *customers* want than what your competitors are doing. Then develop and execute a business model that focuses on delivering what your customers tell you they want.

Cured of CWCS, you'll experience the healthy condition of repeat business from loyal customers you can't run off.

Write this on a rock ... CWCS in a big business is inefficient and ugly; but in a small business, it's terminal.

The nature of humans

Spend time in the marketplace and you'll experience close encounters of the third kind with the most interesting species in all nature: human beings. And just as we've learned about the nature of other animals, we also know much about human nature.

In many ways, the nature of humans isn't any different from other animals: All need to breathe, eat, drink, procreate, and survive.

But there's something that clearly sets human beings apart from all other fauna: sentience. And one of the manifestations of being self-aware is that beyond whatever is needed, humans also *want*.

The most essential thing small business owners must understand about the nature of those very important humans— our customers—is the difference between what they *need* and what they *want*.

Tires or time

All humans who own automobiles will need to buy new tires at some point. But what they *want* is to not blow a whole day finding and acquiring them.

So if you're in the tire business, should you advertise your tires, which are commodities and, therefore, very much like those of your competitors? Or should you develop a marketing program that anticipates when your customers' tires need replacing, and handles that project for them, including pick-up and delivery? How about this tag line: "New tires *and* your Saturday back."

House or home

Basically the hairless weenies of the animal kingdom, human

beings need shelter. But what human customers *want* is a home, not a house.

So if you're a realtor, should you focus your assistance on the obligatory list of a house's features, or how the physical setting and interior space fit what you've learned is your customers' sense of what a home is? Try this on:

"Mrs. Johnson, countertops can be replaced. What I want to know is how much will you enjoy the sun rising over that ridge as you have your first cup of coffee every morning?"

Manna or memories

Humans, like thousands of other warm-blooded species, need to eat every day, whether they get to or not. But only humans *want* to dine.

...beyond whatever is needed, humans also want.

So if you own a fine dining restaurant, do you emphasize the food that will be soon forgotten, or the atmosphere that can create a memory? Check this out:

"Long after you've forgotten how wonderful our food is, you will still remember that table for two in the corner, or the booth next to the fireplace."

In the 21st century marketplace, the difference between delivering what customers want and trying to sell them stuff you think they need is, as Mark Twain said, "like the difference between lightning and a lightning bug."

Write this on a rock ... Let the Big Box competitors give humans what they need. The only way small businesses can survive in a global marketplace is to do what we do better than anyone else: Find out what customers *want* and then deliver it!

A time for change

There is a time for everything, and a season for every purpose under heaven.

On its face, this well-known King Solomon wisdom, from the 3rd chapter of Ecclesiastes, delivers hopeful encouragement. But implicit in this passage is a somewhat hidden and often troublesome paradox: A time for everything also implies nothing can be forever, and therefore, change is inevitable.

In the abstract, we accept the reality of change. But in practice, we often regard it like the medicine we know we need, but don't want to take. And knowing change is inevitable doesn't make the pill sweeter.

In the marketplace, it was challenging enough to implement change when we had the expectation of not having to do it again anytime soon. But in the 21st century, the bitter pill of change has acquired an unfortunate new characteristic: a frighteningly short duration.

Make change an abiding element

Organizations that will enjoy consistent success in the future will make change an abiding element in their business model, rather than an intrusion to "the way we've always done things." They'll create a culture and environment where change can occur whenever necessary, without creating a casualty list.

Rick Maurer, author of *Beyond the Wall of Resistance*, conducted a survey of organizations that have implemented change. He identified these four things they did to create a culture compatible with change, which are followed by my comments.

1. Make a strong case.

Maurer found that "when change was successful, 95% of the stakeholders saw a compelling need to change."

Change must be accompanied by evidence of its importance. If you can't make the case, either you haven't communicated effectively, haven't done your homework, or it's not the right thing to do—yet.

2. Establish the vision.

Maurer's research indicated 71% of successful changes happened "when people understood the vision of the project."

Clearly, stakeholders will support a new direction better if they can understand the long-term benefits of the change.

3. Sustain the changes.

Failed changes reported to Maurer indicated the primary reason was "leadership's inability to sustain the change."

Leading a successful change isn't a sprint; it's a marathon. It takes time and must endure pressure from many sources. Sustaining change may be the greatest test of leadership.

4. Anticipate maintenance.

Maurer found that managers who attended to the first three areas had the least concerns with the fourth. But all managers must recognize that it's not the nature of change to be self-perpetuating.

Knowing change is inevitable doesn't make the pill sweeter.

Finally, hundreds of human behavioral studies have established that when something positive (or negative) is expected, that's what is likely to happen. It's called the Pygmalion Effect and it can be very powerful—either way.

If we can help our people expect something positive in the changes we're proposing, the outcome probably will be.

Write this on a rock ... The inevitability and velocity of change makes the ability to lead and maintain it an essential management skill.

Consider teleworking

A small business is a lot like a high school football team: talented and courageous players, but with limited depth on the bench, everyone has to play more than one position.

So what do you do when a key employee tells you that, due to circumstances beyond his control, he is now required to stay at home at least part of the work week?

If you don't want to lose a valuable team member, the 21st century answer to this management challenge is teleworking.

Teleworking—where an employee works full- or part-time off-site, usually from home—is becoming much more prevalent in the marketplace. In truth, the need to be able to work off-site isn't new, but only in the past few years have the technological tools been available to make teleworking a viable management option.

And as more and more business owners and executives realize that all work in the 21st century doesn't have to be done under their roof, teleworking has become more acceptable as a management practice—and a valuable alternative to losing a key employee.

Teleworking works

Here are some thoughts on how to establish and execute a teleworking relationship.

The first step is to sit down with a prospective teleworking employee and find out how much work can realistically be done off-site. Then determine how the off-site and on-site schedule would be coordinated. If the answer is acceptable to both parties, make sure everyone has a clear understanding about the schedule, work guidelines and expectations.

Next step—the tools. Get your teleworker a notebook computer (which will allow work to be taken back and forth) and pay for a broadband Internet connection at his or her home. With the new notebook PCs and telecommunication capabilities, often the only difference between a teleworker and any other employee is that teleworkers aren't in plain sight.

Also, you may have to provide your teleworker with furniture that will make his or her home office as productive as possible.

Next, talk with your other employees about why this step is being taken so they can support the new plan. If handled properly, I predict you'll get major points for being such a cool 21st century manager.

Finally, execute your teleworking plan with the knowledge that all parties will benefit from this new working arrangement. You should also anticipate the need to make adjustments, so schedule a periodic review with your teleworker to discuss progress and modifications.

Technology has made teleworking possible.

By the way, if you have trouble imagining having an employee who's not under your roof, here's how to get over it: Think about how many hours a week your key employees are in your building without you actually seeing them. I'll bet that number will surprise you.

And it might make you feel better knowing that the teleworking model is being implemented by small businesses just like yours every day.

Write this on a rock ... Don't lose a key employee because you didn't consider teleworking as an option.

Looking for answers

This is a story about three small business owners and a wise man named Luther.

Oh, by the way, Luther is a janitor, and a wise man.

On Mondays...

...Luther cleans the offices at National Supply Co., Inc. Sometimes he talks with the founder, Mr. Gilbert.

One Monday afternoon Mr. Gilbert said, "Luther, I don't know how long I can survive."

"What's wrong, Mr. G.?" Luther asked.

"It's those Big Box competitors. I've looked under every rock for ways to lower our prices and increase advertising, but I just can't compete with those guys," said Mr. Gilbert.

"Maybe you're looking in the wrong place," Luther said.

"What do you mean?" Mr. Gilbert asked.

Then Luther said, "Those big competitors will always be with us. Why don't you emphasize the value of the human connection and customized service that only a small business can deliver? Those two things alone are worth more than anything the giant companies could ever offer."

On Wednesdays...

...when Luther cleans the offices at Central Data Corp., he often visits with the owner, Sarah.

"Luther, I always assumed my kids would take over my business, but now, it doesn't look like that's going to happen," Sarah lamented one day.

"Why aren't they interested in the business?" Luther asked.

"I don't know. I've shown them the opportunity, and how profitable the business can be. What else can I do?" said Sarah.

"Maybe you're asking them to look in the wrong place," Luther suggested.

"What do you mean?" Sarah asked.

Then Luther said, "Sarah, I've noticed how much you love what you do, even when times were tougher and things weren't so rosy. From what I've seen, being an entrepreneur is as much about nourishing the spirit as growing the bank account. Help them think about that."

On Fridays...

...Luther cleans the offices at Westco Dynamics, Inc. Mr. West usually talks with Luther for a few minutes, but recently he seemed pensive.

"Maybe you're looking in the wrong places."

"Luther, my family was so poor that we struggled just to survive. When I left home, I vowed never to be that unhappy again," Mr. West said.

"Mr. West, it sounds like you've got something stuck in your craw," Luther observed.

"Aw, it's nothing. It's just that, with all my money and stuff, I still can't stop looking for ways to make sure I'll never be poor again," Mr. West said.

"Maybe you're looking in the wrong place," said Luther.

"What do you mean?" Mr. West asked.

Then Luther said, "You've been motivated by the fear of being poor instead of the joy of creating something from nothing. Try finding happiness in knowing that you provide valuable products and services for your customers, and jobs and income for your employees and their families. Remember, money and stuff only give you options, not happiness."

Write this on a rock ... When you're looking for answers, make sure you look in the right places.

The Field of Dreams myth

In the 1989 movie, *Field of Dreams*, the lead character, Ray Kinsella, is a corn farmer who hears a voice that causes him to do strange things.

Kinsella, played by Kevin Costner, first hears the voice say, "If you build it, he will come." And even though he doesn't yet know who "he" is, Kinsella determines that "it" is a baseball field, which he actually builds and which, incredibly, attracts a bunch of dead baseball players.

Field of Dreams is a wonderful feel-good movie because in the end, everything turns out well for the Kinsella family. But this flick is based on fantasy and, consequently, it is best enjoyed by suspending all attachment to reality.

The field of dreams myth

Unfortunately, some entrepreneurs believe the Field of Dreams Myth, which is, "If I build it they will come." They think that by merely building "it" (which is a business), not only will "they" (the customers) come, but they will consistently do so and in sufficient numbers to insure the success of that business.

This will be on the test:

In the 21st century marketplace, "if I build it they will come," is a business strategy based on fantasy, and the business equivalent of a death wish.

Any questions?

From time immemorial right up until somewhere around 1990, the Field of Dreams strategy was never a very intelligent way to start a business. It's always been prudent to survey the market to identify how that pie is being carved up by the current participants, plus how prospective customers will accept the entry of your product or service.

But prior to 1990 it wasn't difficult to identify all your

competitors, which you could probably count on your fingers. Today, you couldn't do it with a supercomputer.

Every day of the 21st century, our customers have a virtually infinite number of purchasing options through the many new competitive models in the traditional marketplace, plus the thousands of options available through the virtual channels made possible by the Internet. So as you develop your 21st century business strategy, the Field of Dreams voice in your head should be saying:

If I build it, they will come, is a dangerous myth.

"If you build it, customers will only come the first time if you offer a compelling value proposition that clearly and quickly identifies what's in it for them. And even then, they won't come back unless you make sure their experience is so exceptional that they choose to forsake all other options."

Go the distance

There is one message the voice in Ray Kinsella's head told him that tracks perfectly with our new Field of Dreams business strategy. When Kinsella was up against his most challenging obstacles, the voice said, "Go the distance."

You must go the distance to determine who your customers are, what they want, why they're doing business with you today, and what they require to come back tomorrow.

Write this on a rock ... All small business owners must understand the 21st century Field of Dreams strategy and be prepared to go the distance to execute it.

Red herrings are for foxhunts

For centuries, English foxhunters dragged a red herring in front of their hounds in order to distract them from the scent of the little furry guy.

In time, this practice produced the metaphorical "red herring," which is an attempt to win an argument or negotiation by diverting attention from the real issue at hand.

Introducing a red herring in a discussion or negotiation can be a handy defensive tactic. But sometimes we use personal red herrings, which is when we lie to ourselves.

Personal red herrings

It's one thing to use red herrings with others as a communication tactic. But when we use them on ourselves, it's unproductive at best and destructive at worst.

Shakespeare addressed this issue five centuries ago in perhaps his most famous play. Sharing his wisdom in Act I, Scene III, of *Hamlet*, Polonius said, "This above all: to thine own self be true."

If you can't be true to yourself, you can't be true to your dream. And a false dream is an entrepreneurial atomic meltdown waiting to happen.

Perhaps the most difficult challenge you'll face is knowing when to continue to believe in whatever you're working on, and when it's time to move on. And the dilemmas on these horns could range from a small piece of your plan, all the way to the actual validity of your vision and viability of the dream upon which you've staked your future.

One of my mentors helped me learn how to face these "go—no go" decisions by asking this question: "Do you have a fighting chance, or just a chance to fight?"

The key to success in business, and indeed in life, may be as simple as knowing the answer to that question.

Check your position

One way to tell if you're dragging a stinking fish across the trail of your own dream is by checking your position. Here are three examples:

1. Have you conducted enough due diligence to find out if your plan has a reasonable chance of being successful? If not, telling yourself things will work out is a red herring.

2. Is your activity resulting in *any* success? If nothing is working, convincing yourself that you just need to work harder is masking reality.

3. Are your assumptions performing? If you are only consuming resources without creating opportunity, you must tell yourself the truth: You're not on the right trail—yet.

The whole truth

Do you have a fighting chance, or just a chance to fight?

When even small successes can be found mixed in with the failures, you may have a vision merely in need of adjustments, and worthy of extra effort.

But in order to evaluate all of this, small business owners need all the facts they can get their hands on. And they need the truth from all parties—especially themselves.

The marketplace is formidable enough. Use red herrings for foxhunting and negotiating, not on yourself.

Write this on a rock ... "This above all: to thine own self be true."

Negotiating for success

Negotiating is a process of communication between two or more parties to reach an agreement on future behavior — like when you're purchasing a business, leasing an office, hiring an employee, selling a product, or trying to get a two-year-old to take one more bite of peas.

Let's look at the two operative words in that definition— process and communication.

Process

Conducting a negotiation is more like running a marathon than sprinting. It's a process that takes time and usually involves multiple steps.

By accepting this reality in the beginning, you'll set yourself up to be more patient, and therefore, more effective. Remember, impatience by one party is the other party's best negotiating leverage.

Communication

In addition to the spoken word, there are many other ways to communicate in a negotiation. Punctuality, appearance, organization, and attention to detail, for example, are all types of communication. You even communicate *in absentia* with the quality of the documents you produce.

Never underestimate the heightened awareness of every aspect of a negotiation. The slightest nuance, gesture, or facial expression can mean something. Make sure that all of your communication with the other party contributes to your negotiating objectives.

Now let's look at three critical questions to ask yourself before any negotiation.

1. What do I want?

This might seem silly, but make sure you have this conversation with yourself. If you don't know exactly what you want, how will you know when to stand firm and when to give something away?

And if the other party senses you're not focused, he or she will either disengage or view you as weak prey and take advantage. Either way, you lose.

2. Why should the other party negotiate with me?

If a genie grants you one wish prior to starting a negotiation, ask him what motivates the other party. Armed with that important perspective, you can get the other information you'll need in due time.

3. What are my options?

The best way to get what you want in any negotiation is if you don't have to do the deal. If you have an alternative to what's on

A negotiation is more like running a marathon than sprinting.

the table, your ability to walk away from a deal that isn't moving in your favor will be greatly improved. It doesn't have to be perfect—just an alternative.

By the time you find out what the other party is willing to do, your second choice might start looking pretty good. And merely knowing you're in a position to walk away will make you a better negotiator.

Don't fall in love

Whatever you do, don't fall in love with any deal unless you want to make the other party's day. Love is for lovers—this is business.

Write this on a rock ... In business, everything is negotiable. The question is, are you a capable negotiator?

Focus on politics

How can politics be an operating fundamental? Well, how is your business affected when Congress raises the minimum wage, or an agency imposes a new regulation?

Politics definitely influences your small business. Your choice is either contribute to the debate and help shape laws and policies that affect you, or take what you're given by policy makers who could rightly assume you don't care.

For starters, know who your local, state and federal elected representatives are, and contact them about the issues that are important to you.

Every year these officials participate in passing laws and statutes, plus establish regulations and mandates that affect your business. Unfortunately, too often the effect is negative.

Too many politicians haven't made a payroll

Here are two reasons why it's naïve to expect policy makers to act intuitively in the best interest of small business:

1. Far too many have never made a payroll, and consequently, know little or nothing about the challenges small business owners face.
2. The political voice of small business is not as loud and influential as other groups.

Your involvement will help fix this disparity. But in addition to identifying small business issues to policy makers, we also have to educate them about those issues.

For Congressional representatives, a good place to start is to find out how they voted on laws that affect small business. Congratulate them on a good small business voting record. If the record is bad, remind them that you're not happy about it. You can find the voting records at the two Web sites below.

Some issues you know, like lower taxes, fewere regulations and industry specific issues.

Some issues are more obscure, like laws that lead to regulations and mandates that insidiously suck precious working capital out of small businesses.

Did you know that, according to the U.S. Small Business Administration, regulatory compliance costs each small business over $7,000 per employee annually? That's almost twice as much as large businesses. Need any more reasons to get involved?

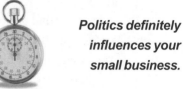

Politics definitely influences your small business.

Find, support, and participate with groups that track key small business policy issues, and who defend and advocate for small businesses at all government levels. Here's the short list, including Web sites:

- Your local Chamber of Commerce
- U.S. Chamber of Commerce, www.uschamber.com
- National Federation of Independent Business www.nfib.com
- Small Business & Entrepreneurship Council www.sbecouncil.org
- Your industry's trade group.

America needs more people involved in the public policy debate who have made a payroll. If you can't run yourself, support those who know first-hand about the challenges you face in your small business.

Write this on a rock ... The choice is yours: Participate in the policy debates affecting your business, or take what you're given by policy makers who will rightly assume that you don't care.

What really matters

I saw a werewolf drinking a pina colada at Trader Vic's; His hair was perfect.

This is one of my favorite lyrics by one of my favorite songwriters. It's from the 1978 song, "Werewolves Of London," by that great 20th century poet, sage, and malcontent, Warren Zevon.

If poets were punctuation, Warren Zevon was a great big bold, in-your-face exclamation point, in a world where most of his kind were common periods and commas. Sadly, this important punctuation passed from our prosaic world at the much-too-young age of 56.

Having penned songs like the never more ironic, "Life'll Kill Ya," it's difficult to connect Zevon's life to the world of small business—with one exception: He was an independent artist who, like most small business owners, worked without a net, passionately creating his products, in hopes of finding customers who would appreciate and pay for his wares.

Enjoy every sandwich

Diagnosed with cancer, Zevon knew his time on this earth was limited. In preparing for death, Zevon had one very important thing to say to us, and I think, especially to small business owners.

Being interviewed by David Letterman a few weeks before he died, Letterman asked what Zevon had learned about life. Looking straight through the camera lens into every soul watching, he said, "Enjoy every sandwich!"

Zevon didn't mean life is short, so go make more sales. This man, whose life's work was the definition of sardonic, was saying, "This going on just in: You're not going to live forever!"

"Enjoy every sandwich," was Zevonese for "Slow down to

the speed of life! Hug your kids! Listen to a bird! Contemplate a cloud!"

In a former life, I counseled several small business owners who were going through difficult times in their businesses. Often the circumstances would be so desperate and the prognosis so dire that the persons on whom these business's buck stopped would be consumed by stress to the point of being unable to function.

Having been there myself, and calling upon what I had learned about what's really important in life, I would ask this question: "How are your children?"

With a look that screamed, "Haven't you been listening to me? I'm about to lose everything I've worked for!" they would invariably ask, "What?!"

When asked the same question the second time, they would just as invariably say, "They're fine. Why are you asking me that?"

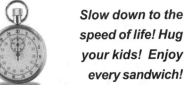

Slow down to the speed of life! Hug your kids! Enjoy every sandwich!

To which I would respond, "Does anything else *really* matter?"

Small business owners can get so wrapped up in their business that they risk losing their grip on the things that *really* matter in life: health, happiness, relationships with family and friends who love them—even their own soul.

Professional success is important—but not at the expense of love. Financial security is a good thing—but it's not more important than health.

And all the credentials in the world can't begin to move the scales when weighed against having joy in your life.

Write this on a rock ... Life is short—enjoy every sandwich! Thanks, Warren.

Sources

Ciancutti, M.D., Arky and Stedling, Thomas L.,
Ph.D., *Built On Trust*, Contemporary Books,
Chicago, 2001.

Freedman, Alan, Glossbrenner, Alfred and Glossbrenner, Emily
(eds), *The Computer Desktop Encyclopedia*, AMACOM,
New York, 1998,

Martin, Steve, *Creative Approaches For The Cost Effective
Organization*, Business Solutions – The Positive Way,
Williamsville, NY, 1999.

Maurer, Rick, *Beyond The Wall Of Resistance*, Bard Press,
Austin, 1996.

Misner, Ivan, Ph.D. and Morgan, Don, Ph.D., *Masters of
Networking*, Bard Press, Atlanta, 2000.

Naisbitt, John, *Megatrends*, Warner Books, New York, 1984.

ODonohue, John, *Eternal Echoes*, HarperCollins, New York,
1999.

Sherman, Andrew, *Franchising & Licensing*, American
Management Association, New York, 1999.

———, *Raising Capital*, American Management Association,
New York, 2003.

Smith, Adam, *The Wealth Of Nations* (originally published in
Scotland, 1776), Random House, New York, 1994.

Congratulations

You are a member of The Small Business Advocate community by the fact that you own this book.

You can record your membership by sending an email to dsb@jbsba.com, to receive advance notice of, and a member discount on Jim's next book.

Another way to join our community is to subscribe to Jim's free electronic NEWSLETTER from the Web site, www.SmallBusinessAdvocate.com. And be sure to check out Jim's Blog on the Web site, or directly at JimsBlog.biz.

You are now connected to the thousands of entrepreneurs in Jim's worldwide listening and reading audience. Plus you're only one degree of separation away from the hundreds of members of The Small Business Advocate Brain Trust, the largest community of small business experts in the world.

Tune in to Jim's show on the radio or the Internet for a direct connection at www.SmallBusinessAdvocate.com.

Welcome aboard.

About the author

Jim Blasingame is the creator and award-winning host of the nationally syndicated weekday radio/Internet talk show, The Small Business Advocate, on the air since 1997. He conducts over 1,000 live interviews every year.

Jim has assembled the largest community of small business experts in the world—which he calls the Brain Trust—and he interviews one of them every half hour on his show.

Now heard in dozens of radio markets across the U.S., Jim is also considered one of the pioneers in on-demand audio streaming. He was the first to offer small business content on the Internet, live and archived. Jim also has a daily feature, *The Small Business Minute*, on XM Satellite Radio.

The U.S. Small Business Administration named Jim the 2002 Small Business Journalist of the Year. In 2003, 2004 and 2005, *TALKERS Magazine* recognized Jim as a member of the the "Heavy Hundred," the 100 most important talk show hosts in America.

FORTUNE Small Business magazine identified Jim as one of the 30 most influential people in America representing small business interests, and one of America's top small business resources.

Jim has been a small business owner since 1989, when he founded his business consulting company. Today he's the president of Small Business Network, Inc., a media company that produces and distributes more multi-media small business content than any other person or organization in the world, with the flagship brand being *The Small Business Advocate Show*.

His career has included tenures with Sears, Xerox, and the U.S. Army. He has conducted business at all levels of the U.S. marketplace, as well as internationally.

In addition to being a professional speaker and trainer, Jim is also a prolific writer. Combining his syndicated newspaper column, his Blog, JimsBlog.biz, his ezine, The Small Business Advocate *NEWSLETTER*, plus his books and dozens of electronic and print publications, Jim cranks out over 100,000 words per year on small business issues.

When he's not working ...

...Jim is a Rotarian (past-president, 15-year perfect attendance), an ardent supporter of Chambers of Commerce (member of his own Chamber since 1977 and past board member), and teaches an adult Sunday School class (18 years).

His greatest successes are: a daughter who is a Registered Nurse and the mother of Jim's two grandsons (Jim has taken "obnoxious grandparent" to a new level), and a son who is a police officer and staff sergeant in the U.S. Marine Reserves.

Jim is a licensed pilot with instrument and multi-engine ratings. He owns a set of golf clubs, plays the guitar for his own amazement and aspires to be a gourmet chef.

Jim is a high energy speaker ...

... and is available to deliver keynote addresses at your meetings and conferences, as well as emcee and panel moderating duties. For more information, contact Davonna Hickman, Vice President, Small Business Network, Inc.: 888-823-2366 or email dsb@jbsba.com.

Three Minutes
To Success

...is an excellent and timeless merchandising gift for customers and clients. We will customize your copies of Jim's book with a foil label on the cover, with your organization's name printed on it, such as...

**Compliments of
ABC Consulting**

Plus we have other customizing options to offer and will consider your ideas.

For quantity discount pricing, customizing and special fulfillment options, please contact SBN Books.

Toll Free 888-823-2366
Fax 256-760-0027
Email .... mail@sbnbooks.com

Use this contact information for single orders as well, or go to www.sbnbooks.com to order online.